SCULPTURE IN WOOD

SCULPTURE IN WOOD

FERELYTH AND BILL WILLS

*With over 300 black-and-white illustrations
and 8 pages of colour plates*

*All photographs and drawings are by the
authors unless otherwise indicated*

DAVID & CHARLES
NEWTON ABBOT LONDON
ARCO PUBLISHING COMPANY, INC.
NEW YORK

To John Skeaping

This edition first published in 1975
in Great Britain by
David & Charles (Holdings) Limited,
Newton Abbot, Devon,
in the USA by
Arco Publishing Company, Inc.,
219 Park Avenue South,
New York, NY 10003

0 7153 6490 1 (Great Britain)
Arco Order Number 3665
LCCCN 74-25009
© Ferelyth and Bill Wills 1975

Printed photolitho in Great Britain
by Ebenezer Baylis & Son Limited
The Trinity Press, Worcester, and London

CONTENTS

ACKNOWLEDGEMENTS

We would like, first, to thank John Skeaping for the years at the LCC Central School of Arts and Crafts. His teaching has provided the basis for this book.

We hope that we have remembered accurately, and have repeated clearly, the fundamental principles and the technical advice which he gave so generously: also that we have managed to reflect his positive attitude towards the material, and towards the idea of truly three-dimensional shape.

His sculptures in Lincoln Cathedral were photographed specially for this book with the kind permission of the Dean of Lincoln and of King's College Cambridge. The three figures were commissioned by King's College for the Chapel, to fill the empty niches in the Edwardian reredos by Detmar Blow. They were subsequently replaced by the great Rubens altarpiece 'The Adoration of the Magi', and are at present on loan to the Cathedral.

The photograph of John Skeaping's 'Horse' was provided by the Tate Gallery, London; as was that of 'Hollow Form with White' by Barbara Hepworth.

We are especially grateful to Lord Clark for permission to reproduce his photograph of the sculpture 'Composition', by Henry Moore, which is in his collection; to the Ashmolean Museum, Oxford, for their photograph of the model adze from Thebes and for permission to use the photograph of the head 'Coloured Girl from Massachusetts' by Dora Clarke, and to the artist herself for providing this and the other photographs of her work: 'Head' in elm, owned by Mrs T. H. Clarke, and 'Resting Boy', owned by Mrs G. Ahern.

We thank John Skelton for his photographs of his own work; Thalia Polak, George Taylor, John Thorpe and Ken Wilkinson for allowing us the pleasure of photographing their work for inclusion in this book; and those who kindly gave us permission to do the same with works in their possession: Miss M. Beckett, Miss I. Henstock, Misses G. and J. Wills, Mr and Mrs A. J. Allan, Mr and Mrs H. A. Barker, Mr and Mrs E. Barnsley, Mr and Mrs J. Firth, Mr and Mrs L. Friend, Mr and Mrs C. Fine, Mr and Mrs W. I. and Miss R. Massil, Mr and Mrs D. M. Turner Warwick; also those owners whose names we have been unable to trace.

Very special thanks are due to Pauline and Ray Forster for their part in producing an adze similar to the one described in this book. This adze was the last of a batch specially made to John Skeaping's design, and has been unobtainable since 1946. As a result of the Forster's initiative and Tirantis' co-operation this most useful tool will again be obtainable.

We end with a warm 'thank you' to the many others who have helped us, particularly to our own family and to our friends; to Jean MacGibbon for her encouragement and advice; to Gillian and Jackie Wills for their support and to Lesley Lowe for her help in putting the book together.

Ceremonial adze from the foundation deposits of the Great Temple of Queen Hatsepshut, Thebes 1500 BC. Ashmolean Museum, Oxford

Sculptor's adze, AD 1970

INTRODUCTION

D. S. MacColl, formerly keeper of the Tate Gallery and of the Wallace Collection, says in his book *What is Art?* (1940): 'Art is a way of doing and making things'.

By this 'doing and making' art can be a means of sharing experience, of communicating ideas through the mechanism of the senses.

Rhythm, pattern, texture; these are among the elements which are common to all forms of artistic expression. In addition, each of the senses has its own particular area of awareness.

Painting is the art of sight and of the mind's eye. Music is the art of sound; of the mind's ear.

Sculpture is the art of touch; of the mind's hand. To feel something in the hand is to know the reality of it and the true basis of that reality is the material from which it is made.

For this reason wood is an ideal material for sculpture. The beauty of the colours, the contrasts in the grain caused by the natural growth of the tree,

are qualities which become an integral part of the final expression.

In this book we are not showing how wood can be used as a material for the many different forms of art and craft such as constructions or relief sculpture. Constructions can be made of wood but they do not require its special qualities for their impact.

On the other hand, wood is an interesting material for relief sculpture but there must be a compromise in design between the three-dimensional shape and the two dimensions imposed by the depth of the material.

So this book is about one art form only, using the fullest, richest beauty of one material to present the maximum value, in three dimensions, of a shape in space. The starting point here is for the individual to need to share experience by his own way of 'doing and making' things, for it is only through the arts that man can bridge the gap of separateness.

THE MATERIAL

As a material, wood has the advantage of being plentiful and not too expensive, although it can be difficult to find pieces really suitable for sculpture purposes. It does not require a big outlay on special tools or equipment, but it does need sympathetic handling and storage.

Sculpture is the art of conveying an idea by the creation of a three-dimensional shape in space – a shape which must be a compromise between the concept of the sculptor and the nature of the material used. Real understanding of the latter is therefore essential, and in this respect wood is very demanding, since no two pieces are identical, no two species behave in quite the same way, and no single piece is entirely predictable. You need to learn the 'feel' of it, and to develop a feeling for it. Bear in mind that it is, or has been, a living substance: one which has grown and developed with the sole purpose of making an efficient tree; able to survive storm and drought, and to resist attack by animals, insects and fungi.

Alive, it manages remarkably well; after felling it will, slowly, try to acclimatise to its new environment; but, robbed of its living protective system, it will be more prone to damage, and will need help to delay or defeat the natural processes of decay.

The best approach to understanding wood is to consider how it grows.

Among the many useful, available woods the following are shown in this picture:
Imported woods: American box, bubinga, danta, doussie, ebony, hickory, iroko (teak substitute), lignum vitae, mahogany, rosewood, teak;
Home-grown woods: acacia, apple, ash, beech, box, cherry, elm, holly, lime, mulberry, oak, pear, prunus, sweet chestnut, sycamore, walnut, yew.

HOW A TREE GROWS

All timber-producing trees grow in the same way. Special cells at the top and at the tips of branches provide the growth in height or length; growth in diameter is achieved by the 'cambium', a very thin layer immediately beneath the bark. By division of its cells the cambium adds, each year, layers of new wood and new bark over the entire surface of the tree – trunk, branches and twigs alike. The resulting structure of superimposed, and firmly bonded, cone-like sheaths is shown diagrammatically above. For clarity, branches have been omitted. Small twigs occurring in early years usually break off or die, and are covered over by the next year's 'sheath' of new wood.

The new wood – tightly knit fibres lying lengthwise up the tree and along the branches – is called 'sapwood'. At first it is relatively soft, and useless as timber; but as the years go by and successive layers are added, the inner layers of sapwood are converted gradually into the stronger, more durable and useful, heartwood – the biological purpose of which is to support the tree during its long life. Eventually, when the tree is past its prime, the heartwood will start to decay, and to rot away until the tree dies or is blown down. To provide plenty of heartwood, therefore, trees must be well developed, but not over-developed to the point where decay has started.

Section of young Scots fir, showing structure of trunk and branches

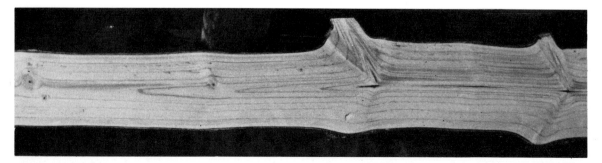

THE STRUCTURE OF WOOD

The cross-section of a recently felled tree shows a series of approximately concentric rings, known as 'annual' or 'growth' rings. These occur because the wood formed in the spring and early summer, when growth is most rapid, is lighter in colour (and also somewhat softer) than that formed more slowly in the autumn, which therefore appears as a darker ring. This colour difference is usually most marked in trees growing in temperate or cold climates, where the seasonal variation is greatest. Sapwood is usually (but not always) lighter in colour than heartwood, although the difference may not be clear until the surface has dried.

The raw food assimilated by the roots of the tree is conveyed upwards, in the form of crude sap, through the outer layers of sapwood to the leaves. Here the crude sap is converted by the action of sunlight into 'elaborated sap', which then descends through the inner layers of the bark and feeds the cambium, enabling it to reproduce its cells by division, forming new wood on the inside and new bark on the outside.

The 'pith', or 'medulla' (Latin, meaning 'heart') serves to conduct the sap only in the first few years of growth; it then dries and hardens, remaining visible, but useless as timber, in the centre of the tree. Conversion of sapwood to heartwood is a gradual process, aided by the 'medullary rays' – thin, plate-like cell structures which lie vertically and radially in the tree. These occur in all trees, but are prominent only in some hardwoods, notably oak and beech.

Sections of Scots fir, showing A bark; B cambium layer; C sapwood; D heartwood; E pith

Oak log, showing medullary rays

HARDWOODS AND SOFTWOODS

The two commonly used classifications of 'hardwoods' and 'softwoods' are misleading. One of them distinguishes between deciduous and evergreen trees; the other between broad-leaved and needle-leaved trees. Neither is accurate. Botanically, the difference lies in the cell structure: that of 'softwoods' being less complex than that of 'hardwoods'.

These terms are a trade convention, and are only a rough guide to the actual hardness of any particular wood. Nevertheless, most of the timbers which best meet the requirements of sculpture – pleasing appearance, ease of working, stability and durability – are classed as 'hardwoods'. One notable exception is yew, which, though technically a 'softwood', is hard, heavy and durable, and finishes well. Softwoods generally are less durable, and the sudden contrasts in hardness of spring and autumn wood make it very difficult to control the surface.

GRAIN

It is the combination of the method of growth – by the annual addition of an extra layer – and the fibrous nature of the substance added which gives to wood its unique characteristic of 'grain', the effects of which are: a very marked difference in strength along, and across, the axis of the tree; and an attractive appearance, or 'figure', to the finished surface after working.

The biological purpose of the heartwood is to support the tree so that growth can continue; therefore it must be very strong, lengthwise, to resist the enormous loads caused by high winds. In normal conditions there is little tendency for the tree to split vertically, and consequently less need for great strength in that direction.

This difference in strength is very important to the sculptor, who must therefore consider carefully the grain direction with relation to intended shape, and vice versa. Sometimes timber can be found with the grain running helpfully; sometimes the lie of the grain will suggest a subject; almost always, some compromise will be necessary to avoid structural weakness in the finished work.

A small strip of softwood (about $\frac{1}{2}$in × $\frac{1}{4}$in) with grain running lengthwise is barely affected by a load of 6lb.

A strip of the same size cut across the grain of the same log only just supports 4lb . . .

. . . and the addition of an extra $\frac{1}{2}$lb is disastrous!

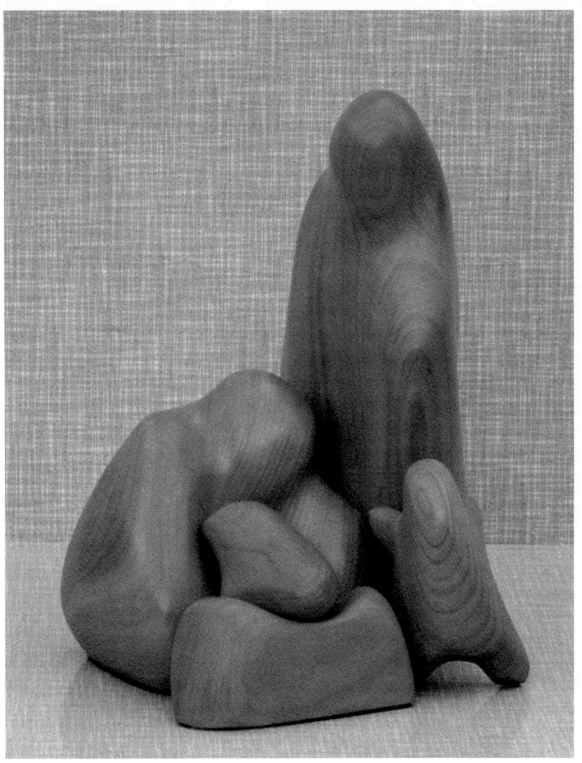

CHERRY *Family Group*

OAK *Sea Bird*

WALNUT *Kitten*

LIGNUM VITAE *Woodland Animal*

YEW *Ginger Cat*

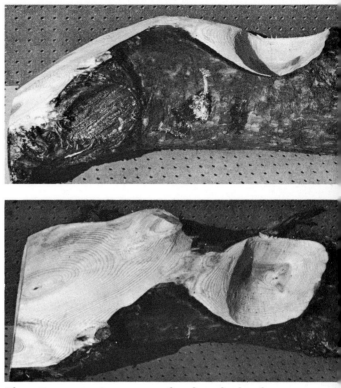

Grain 'figure' is contributed largely by the annual rings, which form a series of approximately concentric 'tubes' up and down the tree, and along the branches.

The pattern appearing on any surface depends, therefore, on how that surface lies in relation to the axis of the tree or branch.

Since wood is composed of tightly knit stringy fibres, clean cutting depends on working in the right direction: that is, 'with' (A) rather than 'against' (B) the grain (*lower right*).

The Scots fir in the illustrations was chosen for clarity, and is a very uncomplicated example. Many timbers are much more difficult to assess, but if the fibrous structure of the material is kept firmly in mind, the right direction for working is usually evident. If it is not, try a cautious cut in the most likely direction, but be prepared to change if necessary. With very difficult woods, particularly those with 'interlocking' grain such as afrormosia (*below*), working almost across the grain reduces the risk of serious damage to the surface.

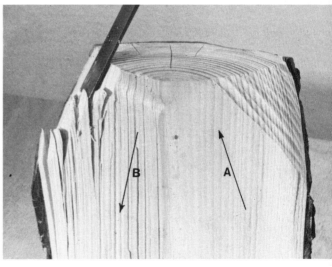

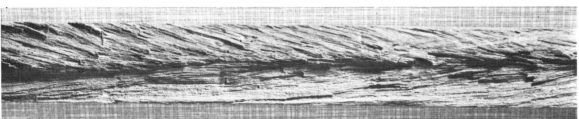

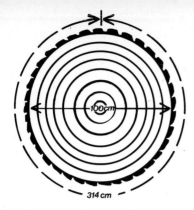

Freshly cut circular log: diameter 100cm, circumference 314cm

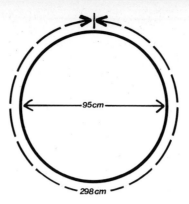

After 5 per cent shrinkage a true circle would measure: diameter 95cm, circumference 298cm.

With a log, however, if the diameter shrinks 5 per cent to 95cm, the circumference shrinks 10 per cent to 282cm, and cannot make up the required 298cm without splitting.

SEASONING, STABILITY AND SHRINKAGE

Newly felled timber contains a large amount of moisture, which must be reduced by 'seasoning' to a proportion suitable for its intended environment. Any further drying or reabsorption of moisture from the air will cause distortion, to a degree depending on the quantity of moisture, and the type of wood, involved: the woods least affected being classed as the most 'stable'.

Shrinkage on drying is unavoidable: it causes many problems, which are aggravated by the fact that the amount of shrinkage varies according to its direction relative to the axis of the tree. Lengthwise (along the grain) it is negligible – usually less than 1 per cent;

across the log through the centre, it is greater – around 2–7 per cent; round the outside (as it were 'parallel' to the growth rings) it is most of all – about 6–15 per cent, or roughly twice the radial shrinkage: it is this last factor that causes the trouble.

One unfortunate result of this uneven shrinkage is that almost any log left 'in the round' will tend to split as it dries – how seriously will depend on the type of wood, where it is stored and how slowly the drying takes place.

With big logs, splitting can be much reduced by halving or quartering as soon as possible after felling; this enables the tensions to be eased by the whole segment changing shape. Another possibility, if the intended shape permits it, is to remove the centre portion of the log, thereby allowing the diameter to shrink more nearly in proportion to the circumference.

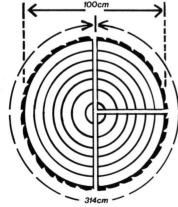

If a large log is halved or quartered soon after felling . . .

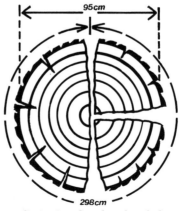

. . . splitting is reduced as the whole segment can distort to ease tension at the circumference.

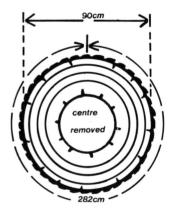

If the centre can be removed, the diameter can shrink to match the circumference.

14

OBTAINING WOOD

For seasoned or part-seasoned wood the most likely sources are the big importers and sawmills. Thickness is the main problem. Merchants seldom stock anything much over 3in, but they do sometimes have odd chunks of hardwood which are unsuitable for conversion into stock sizes. Foreign timbers are too numerous to list here. Any seasoned hardwood is worth trying. If you have any choice avoid (anyway at first) those with interlocking grain, as they are difficult to work.

Of the home-grown timbers, walnut and yew deserve special mention. Sycamore, elm, lime, ash, and fruit woods generally are good; oak is difficult unless really dry. Home-grown stock is rarely fully seasoned; imported woods are usually drier, if only due to the time taken in getting here. If you have storage space, stock up when you can; extra seasoning time at home helps the wood to acclimatise to its new environment.

If you wish to collect locally grown timber, you will need outdoor storage space. Seasoning requires at least one year per inch of thickness. A well-ventilated shed is ideal; failing this, pieces can be covered individually. Logs are best stored on end, clear of the ground (eg on bricks). Keep the tops covered, but allow air to circulate and avoid direct sunlight. After a few months, when obvious sap activity has ceased, part-seal the ends with paint, wax, or petroleum jelly to reduce splitting. The transition from outside to indoors should be as gradual as possible; the aim is slow, even drying. When selecting logs, allow plenty for wastage due to splitting at the ends, and remember that small logs have a large proportion of sapwood.

DEFECTS IN WOOD

Rot or decay Caused by wood-destroying fungi; usually easy to see; will not spread when timber is dry.
Splits, shakes and checks These are all really splits. 'Shakes' (eg heart, star, ring and cup shakes) are internal splits caused by unusual stresses during growth or felling. They usually show only at the ends of logs, but may extend a long way. 'Checks' are small surface cracks caused by too-rapid local drying; if this continues more serious splits will develop: this risk can be reduced by part-sealing the end-grain.
Insect attack Generally known as 'worm'; caused by beetles laying eggs in the timber. These become grubs which eat their way through the wood, eventually emerging to mate and repeat the cycle. The large holes, $\frac{1}{8}$in or more in diameter, occurring in the outside of some tropical woods, are no cause for alarm: they are left by insects which attack only the living tree. Small holes, about $\frac{1}{16}$in diameter, are more likely to indicate danger, particularly if they appear to be recently made, or produce powder when tapped with a hammer.

The safest plan is to cut away all bark (which harbours many pests), rot, and wormy wood before storing, thus reducing the risk of further trouble.

Heart shake

Star shake

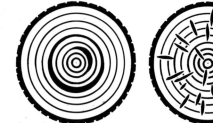
Ring and cup shakes   *Checks*

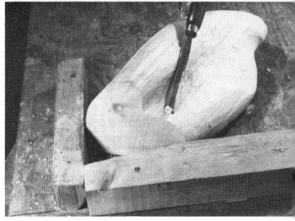

WORKROOM, TOOLS AND EQUIPMENT

Note: on these two pages, numbers in square brackets refer to the diagram below, and page references to examples of use.

WORKROOM   Gentle heating is desirable for comfort and to prevent rusting of tools. Aim at an even temperature and humidity. If the atmosphere is very dry, it is best to keep wood elsewhere between work-sessions to reduce the risk of splitting.

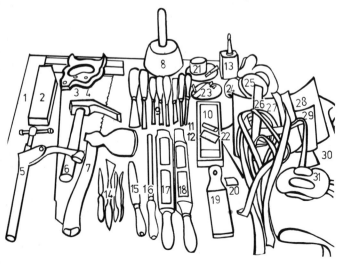

WORKTOPS   You will need a firm bench or table at a convenient height for working when standing: a lower bench in addition is useful for large work, or for working when sitting (p 36).

HOLDING GEAR   A vice is useful, but not essential for sculpture. Work can be steadied against wood blocks nailed or screwed to the bench (*above*) or to a heavy board cramped to the bench. [5] A bench 'holdfast' (p 30) is useful, but note that it requires a hole, at least $\frac{1}{8}$in (3–4mm) larger than its shank, through the bench top. G-cramps may be useful (p 18), particularly if you wish to avoid nailing or screwing to your bench top. A slice of end-grain wood (p 34) makes an ideal chopping board. A leather apron (p 36) and pieces of sacking or corduroy (old trousers) help in holding awkward shapes.

SAWS   [3, 4]   You will need at least one hand-saw. A cross-cut saw (p 30) about 24in, 6 or 7 points per inch, will do most jobs. If you have to do much sawing along the grain it is worth adding a rip saw (p 31), say 26in, 4 points. A coping saw (p 63) is handy for odd small jobs. For unseasoned logs, the 'Bushman' type of saw is best.

ADZE [6]   Wood-sculptor's pattern (p 28), obtainable only from Tiranti (see p 96).

AXE [7]   Almost any hand-axe will do, but the 'Kent' pattern (p 28) is the easiest to keep sharp, due to its short bevel.

MALLET [8]   Stonemason's round pattern preferred (p 19); of beech or lignum vitae.

RASPS   The old-fashioned rasp is not recommended. It has been superseded by the 'Surform' range of files, of which you will need one each: round [16], flat [17] and half-round [18], and spare blades.

FILES [15]   Special files for wood are still made, but engineer's files are almost as good, and much more easily obtained. At least one each, flat and half-round size, to suit work. They are useful on very hard woods, or where the Surform is too bulky. Clean with a file-brush [19] (p 73).

RIFFLERS [14]   A selection of three, say, 6in No 126, 7in No 123, 10in No 125, will give you six differently shaped heads.

ABRASIVES [22, 26–29]   Elektrocut cloth and strip; coarse, medium and fine (p 50). For finishing: 'wet and dry' paper, used mainly dry, can be washed, dried, and re-used. Various grits available (p 52). Ordinary sandpaper is best avoided.

ADHESIVES [23]   For general purposes: Glue-All; Evostik wood adhesive. For special purposes: Araldite or Bostik epoxy resins; these are gap-filling, intensely strong, and dry hard (p 53).

STOPPERS [21]   Various types (pp 53 and 73).

POLISH [25]   Silicone wax polish preferred.

GRINDSTONES   The slow-speed wet sandstone (p 20) is by far the best for woodworking tools, since grinding can continue right up to a new edge without risk of overheating. High-speed emery wheels may be used, but only with great care: apply very light pressure, and dip the tool frequently in water to keep it cool. If the edge starts to turn brown, stop at once; if it turns blue, it has been softened. Either the affected part must be ground away without further overheating, or the tool will require re-hardening and re-tempering. It is safest to stop grinding about $\frac{1}{16}$in (1–2mm) from the edge, and finish by rubbing on an oilstone.

OILSTONES [10]   It saves time to have two stones, one medium and one fine, although you can manage with one if you use a wet sandstone for grinding. A medium Carborundum (artificial) stone is good for quick cutting. For finishing, Arkansas or Washita (natural) stones are the best, but are now almost unobtainable except in small pieces. A fine India (artificial) stone is a good substitute.

SLIPSTONES [11, 12]   Needed for removing the burrs left after stoning. One may be enough provided that its small edge will fit inside your smallest gouge (p 19): Arkansas, Washita, or fine India stone.

OIL [13]   Light machine oil, such as '3 in 1', or special honing fluid. Clean stones occasionally with paraffin.

GOUGES [9]   The basic tools, also the most difficult to sharpen and to keep sharp. Note that carving gouges differ from the ordinary carpenter's pattern in that the blade, particularly of the wider carving gouges, is usually 'fish-tailed' rather than parallel sided. There are many sizes and shapes. The size denotes the width in inches; the number refers to the shape: eg the edge of a $\frac{1}{4}$in no 9 gouge is a semicircle of $\frac{1}{4}$in diameter; that of a 1in no 9 gouge is a semicircle of 1in diameter. The system is universal but there may be slight variations depending upon the manufacturer. Start with a few from the selection below, adding to them as required. It pays to duplicate some of them so that you can keep a few with an extra-long bevel for soft woods or for light finishing cuts.

New gouges are usually supplied roughly ground to shape, but not sharpened: sometimes with, but more often without, handles. It is worth checking this when ordering, as you may need to order handles separately. Some suppliers will fit them for you: if not, this is the first thing to do. Handles should be well finished, to avoid chafing the hands, and are usually fitted with a ferrule to prevent splitting. Boxwood is generally considered the best, but any close-grained hardwood will do. Size and shape are matters of individual preference. In general, a large handle makes control easier and less tiring. For the same

Nos 2   1   5   5   5   6   7   9   18   10

½"   1"   3/8"   5/8"   7/8"   1½"   1¼"   3/4"   7/16"   ¼"

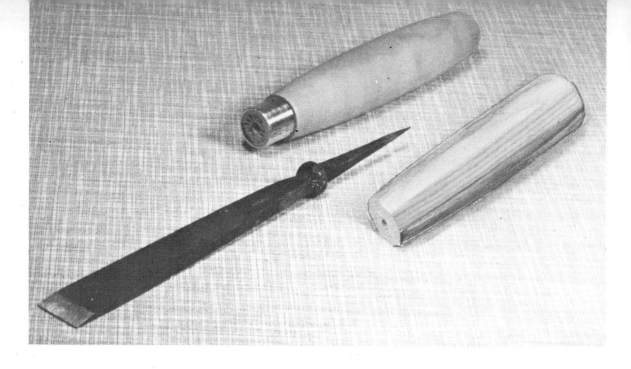

reasons there is much to commend the inexpensive octagonal ash handles, which are comfortable to hold, do not roll off the bench and, despite the absence of a ferrule, will stand a lot of punishment without splitting. Handles are usually supplied with a pilot hole, about $\frac{1}{8}$in diameter, ready-drilled down the centre. If not, make this yourself, taking care to keep straight. Its purpose is to guide the point of the tang during fitting.

The next step is to make the hole in the handle approximately the same shape as, but slightly smaller than, the tang of the gouge. With small gouges this can be done simply by 'working' the handle on to the tang, as in the illustrations.

Now push the handle on, twisting a little each way so that the square edges of the tang scrape away the unwanted wood. Clear the scrapings from the hole frequently.

Hold the gouge by the blade (suitably protected) in a vice, if you have one . . .

. . . by cramping it to the bench . . .

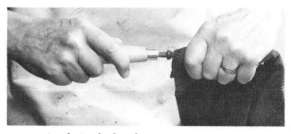

. . . or simply in the hand.

When the end of the handle is about ¼in from the shoulder of the gouge (or about ⅛in in the case of very hard woods such as boxwood), stop twisting, and drive the handle up to the shoulder with a mallet (above). Use care here, and be ready to do more scraping if the fit is too tight. It is essential that the handle makes firm contact with the shoulder, otherwise it will split when in use.

If you have no vice or cramps, support the gouge on a block of scrap wood across the grain (right).

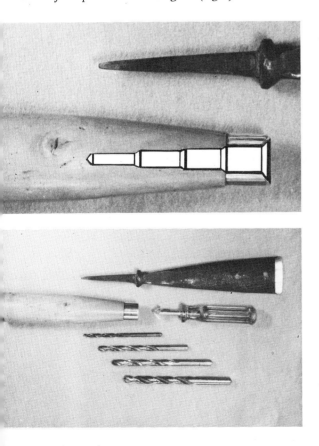

With big gouges, much hard work can be avoided by drilling away some of the excess wood (left and below). Use a series of drills approximating to the thickness of the tang at various depths, starting with the smallest, and remembering that this hole should be a little deeper than the overall length of the tang. It may also be necessary to cut away wood to accommodate the bulge which frequently exists on the tang just below the shoulder (an ordinary countersink bit does this well) to enable the latter to fit snugly against the end of the handle.

Another method is to use the tang of the gouge, made red hot in a gas flame, to burn out the hole in the handle. This works well, but is messy and makes a lot of unpleasant smoke. Great care must be taken to avoid overheating the blade of the gouge, which should be held wrapped in paper, or rag, and cooled frequently with cold water. Quick heating is essential, so that the heat remains localised in the tang. Burn out the hole a little at a time. Stop (as before), just before the shoulder of the gouge reaches the handle, and drive the handle the last ⅛in or so with a mallet.

19

1

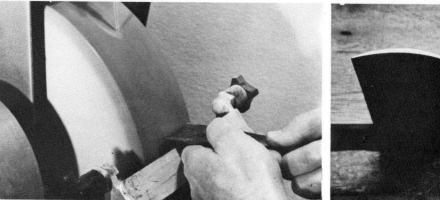

2

A new gouge will probably look like this (above left). The first step is to grind the edge straight.

Hold the gouge against the tool-rest, pointing towards the axle of the grindstone. Whilst grinding, move the gouge to and fro across the full width of the stone to prevent uneven wear (above centre).

When straight, the edge will be uneven in thickness (above) and the bevel uneven in length (below left).

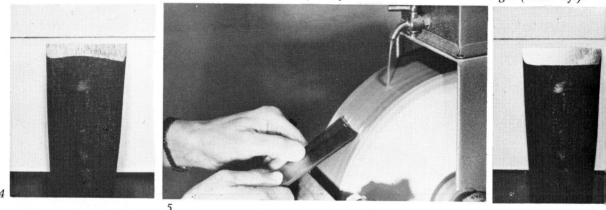

4

5

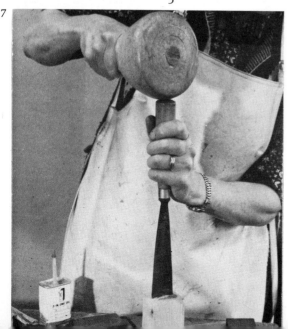

7

Now tilt the gouge (above centre), in order to produce the desired length of bevel (short for hardwoods, longer for soft woods or light finishing cuts) and continue grinding, rotating the gouge as required by its shape and using the full width of the stone. With a wet sandstone, grinding can continue until a sharp edge is produced.

With high speed emery wheels it is safer to stop a little earlier, to avoid risk of overheating when the edge gets thin.

If you continue grinding until a new edge is formed, a 'burr' will develop on the inside curve. This should be removed before proceeding further. A simple method is to tap the gouge into the end grain of a piece of scrap wood (left).

The final working edge is produced by rubbing the gouge on an oilstone (above). Some workers use a 'figure-of-eight' motion, some prefer to work in straight lines along the stone; use whichever method you find the easiest. The important points are: keep the angle constant, rotating the gouge as necessary to sharpen the whole bevel, and try to use the whole surface of the stone. The final aim is an even, sharp edge, an even bevel and an evenly worn stone. The latter should be lubricated with a thin oil, or a special honing fluid such as 'Razedge'.

When sharpening is complete, there should be a small burr right round the inside lip of the gouge. This should be removed by rubbing with a suitable oilstone 'slip', which must be kept flat against the inside surface of the gouge (above).

For very small gouges, very thin slipstones are needed (below). The curvature of the slipstones must be at least a little sharper than that of the gouge. Any tiny traces of burrs may be removed either on a leather strop or, as before, by tapping the gouge into end grain.

Note (above) that sharp edges cannot be seen, since there is no surface to reflect light. If you can see light reflected, the edge is not truly sharp.

(Right) The procedure for sharpening axes and adzes is similar, except that it is easier to hold the tool, suitably supported, on the bench, and rub with the oilstone.

THE BASIC SHAPE

Any one view of it should seem inadequate in itself, the design being completed only when all views of the whole shape have been appreciated.

The eye cannot see a solid shape as a whole. It can only see what is this side of the outline and guess what is beyond or take time to look round and round until the whole shape is appreciated. But if you hold something in your hand you will know what shape it is.

When you have an idea for a piece of sculpture you should be able to feel the shape of it in your mind's hand, just as, feeling for something familiar in your pocket, you would know when you had found it.

When you are making a piece of sculpture or when you are looking at someone else's work, consider it first as a shape in space, asking, 'Is it a good shape or not?' Good and bad in this sense is not entirely a matter of taste or fashion: the first essential of a good shape is that it must be a satisfactory design, or pattern, in all three dimensions.

Whether it is a group of figures, a portrait head or a large abstract sculpture, there should never be any point at which you could remove some part of it and still have a satisfactory design remaining.

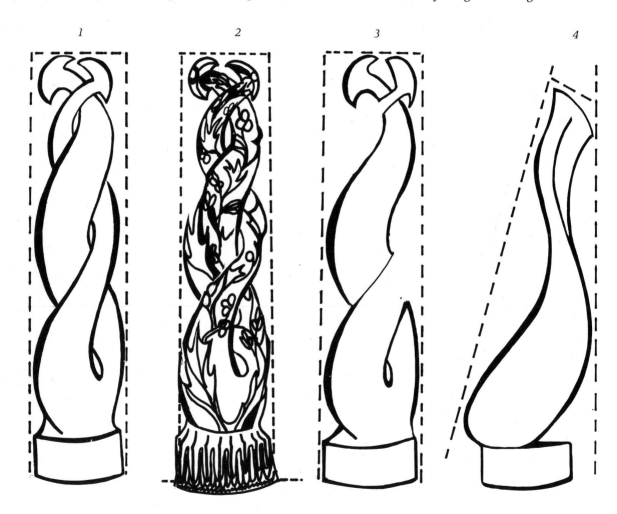

1 In spite of all the twisting and turning, the overall shape of this design is a simple cylinder.

2 No matter how complicated the surface carving may be, the basic shape is still only a cylinder.

Even when part of the design is removed, the basic shape is the same.

To make the shape interesting, the direction of the whole mass must vary in all three dimensions.

If you find it difficult to imagine a shape in three dimensions, think of something you know well; for instance, an ordinary loaf of bread.

Imagine yourself cutting it into slices and see what shape each flat slice would be and how it would differ from the one beside it. Then, if you stand the slices together again, you will be able to appreciate the whole shape.

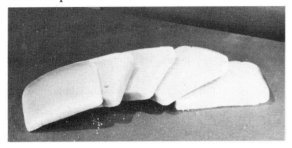

The slices of a dull shape will all be alike; there will be change in two dimensions perhaps, but not in three.

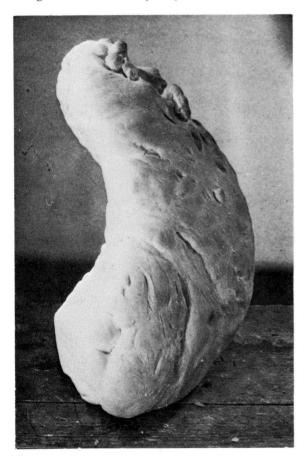

The slices of an interesting shape will all be different; some areas growing larger through the thickness of the slices and some even disappearing altogether. The weight of the mass has changed in emphasis from one part of the shape to another.

To be interesting a shape must have life. It need not be 'life-like' which is a question of subject and preference, nor need it be a kind of magic. Life in art is a matter of design.

The essential quality of life is movement. When you talk of movement in a painting, you mean, really, the movement of the eye across the surface of the picture.

The eye is lazy and it will follow the easy way, the straight lines, the shallow curves, the obvious changes in tone and colour. It is the rhythm of this movement of the eye across the picture that makes the picture seem alive.

The same thing applies to sculpture but in three dimensions. In this case it is the mind's hand which must move over the surface of the sculpture so that at no time should any surface be satisfactory in itself but should lead the hand further. In this way there is constant movement over the surface of the shape so that it has a vitality of its own.

It is the surface movements and the rhythm of their contrasts that will make your sculpture interesting, whatever the subject may be, so from the very beginning, think of the basic mass of the shape and work to develop the surface movements of your idea.

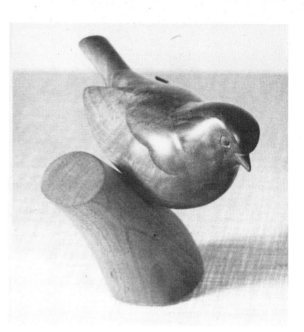

This little robin is full of action and character . . .

. . . but this sleeping figure, although the subject is relaxed, is just as much 'alive' with the balance and counterbalance of the surface movements.

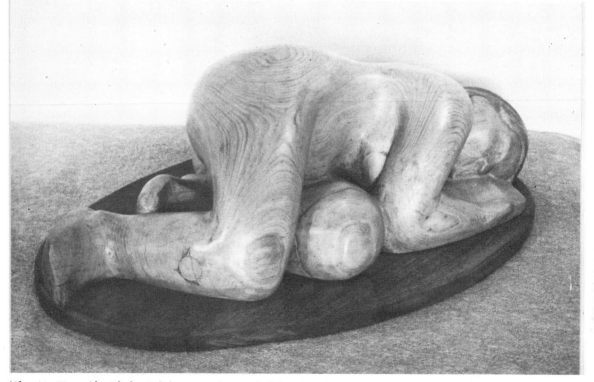

'Sleeping Figure' by Thalia Polak (sweet chestnut); (above) 'Robin' by George Taylor (walnut)

24

It is common practice, when starting a wood-carving, to draw the idea on the surface of the wood . . .

. . . cutting round the outline through the thickness of the block.

The resulting shape will always be square in character . . .

. . . however much you try to round the outside corners or to twist the flat-sided shapes on their axes.

You will soon have to cut away the surfaces you have drawn on and you will lose your bearings from then on.

If the idea is sufficiently clear in your mind, you will not need any drawings, either on the wood or on paper.

What matters is the material you are working in and how you respond to it.

ONE METHOD OF WORKING

There are two ways of setting about making a piece of sculpture: one is to start with an idea; and the other is to start with the material.

I have described the second method with a carving of a small piece of yew, on p 58.

This is the first method.

You have an idea in your mind that you want to express as a shape.

You may see this idea in your imagination as an impression, a character or just as a movement.

Try to visualise the finished shape, turning it over and over in your mind until you can feel it in your hand,

even though, in reality, the final sculpture may be too big to handle in this way.

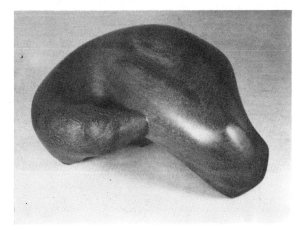

Choose a piece of wood that suits your idea . . .

. . . in colour, character and size.

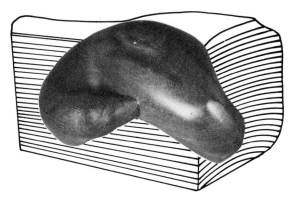

Study the direction of the grain to find the best way of placing your idea within it.

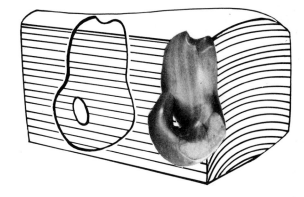

The strength of the wood lies lengthwise along the grain. If a thin part of the design lies across the grain, the wood will break easily at that point.

The contrasts in the figure of the grain will form contour lines giving colour and character to the finished shape.

The shape must suit the material and vice versa. It is this balance between the two, with the constant criticism of the shape as a whole, that forms your piece of sculpture. There will be a battle between these first thoughts and the reality of your piece of wood; a battle that the wood must win if your work is to be not just a skilful carving, but a shape that has grown from within, like the tree from which it came.

27

PREPARING THE WOOD

1 If your choice of wood is from the trunk of a tree, select a part of the trunk where the wood is sound and where the grain is most likely to be interesting; the places where the branches grow from the main stem or from each other.

2 Saw off the piece that you have chosen. It must be larger than the size you have planned for the finished work. The darker area in the picture shows you the proportion of useable heartwood in this particular log. Allow plenty for wastage.

3 Stand the wood on a bench or table top on which you have placed a slice of end-grain wood (like a butcher's block) unless your wood is so big that you must work on it where it stands, either on the soft ground or with the end-grain block underneath.

4 Start to remove the bark, the sapwood and any dead, split or wormy areas, using an axe or an adze.

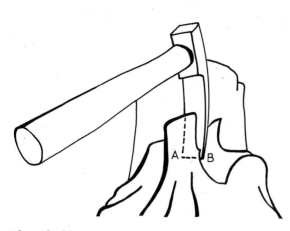

Place the blow accurately so that part A of the blade sinks in between the wood and the bark while part B of the blade splits down the bark itself. In this way the bark will be turned away from the handle of the tool and you will also be able to withdraw the tool for the next blow.

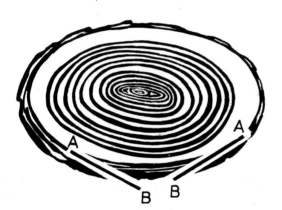

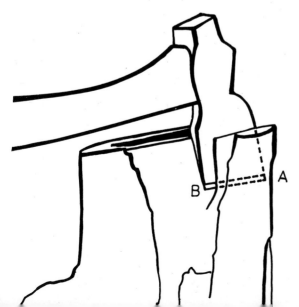

THE CROSS-CUT SAW

Either you have removed the bark and the sapwood from your log, or you are starting with a block of wood which is ready for use.

Visualise your idea within the remaining material and saw off a piece that is only a little larger than the size you have in mind.

Use a cross-cut saw or a rip saw depending on the direction of the grain.

When you are sawing wood that rests on a flat surface (top right), the saw cut will close on the saw and pinch it.

Place a block of wood under the heaviest side of the piece you are sawing, in line with the direction of the saw cut (right). This will stop the pinching.

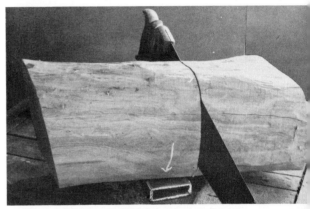

The sawn piece will then fall away, opening the saw cut as it reaches the bottom of the wood.

(Bottom right) This piece has been cut across the grain.

(Below) For small work use a bench hold-fast with a block of wood under the work to prevent the saw from pinching, and a piece of scrap wood under the 'foot' to protect your work from the pressure of the screw.

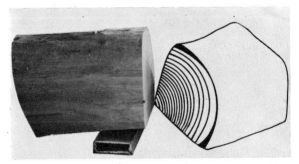

Use a rip saw to saw along the grain.
Place a block of wood underneath, as before, or hold

the wood on the slice of end-grain wood that you have
on the bench.

This has been sawn along the grain.

You may find it easier, particularly with thin bark, as with this piece of yew, to remove it with a gouge and mallet. Cut the bark away in strips using the same method, leaving a little of the tool edge showing out of the wood. This cuts the bark itself while the rest of the tool separates the bark from the wood.

If you are cutting the sapwood with a gouge and mallet, choose a wide shallow gouge and keep it at an angle to the wood, turning the wide shavings away from the hand that holds the gouge.

These two photographs show a large area of dead wood which had to be removed and a deceptive worm hole which, although it looked small to start off with, went across the corner of the wood and had to be cut away.

There may also be an area of wood which has split away from the main block. You can hear when you are carving, or if you tap the wood, that in a certain area the resonant note changes to a flat sound. This means the wood there is either dead or has split loose inside and must be cut away.

If, when you are carving in the direction of the arrow A, the surface looks as it does here, split and torn, you are cutting 'against' the grain. Turn the work the other way up and cut in the direction of the arrow B. You will then be cutting 'with' the grain.

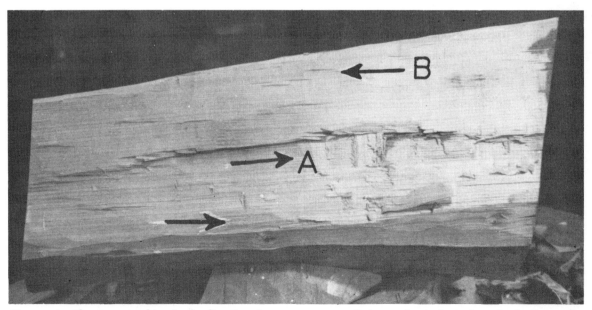

Here again, if you are working in the direction A, you are cutting against the grain. In the direction B you are with the grain. Turn the work round until you are cutting in the right direction. The surface at A is uncontrolled; you do not know how deeply these splits may have torn the wood. The surface at B is controlled. There is no splitting on this surface and the adze cuts are clean, smooth and of an even depth.

CARVING THE BASIC SHAPE

You have visualised your idea and found a piece of wood that suits it in colour, grain and size. You have removed the bark, the dead wood, the worm hole areas and the sapwood, then checked that the size and shape of the remaining clean sound wood is sufficient for your original idea.

Now is the time to visualise clearly the simple basic shape that you require and to start cutting away the unwanted wood.

Use an adze or an axe for this unless the work is very small, in which case you will want to start with a gouge and mallet (p 36).

Think always of the required surface, just beyond the cutting edge of the tool. You will find that by concentrating on this area, rather than on the head of the tool, you will soon be able to cut accurately and to control the surface exactly as you wish.

Stand your work on the slice of end-grain wood on the bench so that the tool can cut downwards, with the grain of your wood, until it meets the end grain of the slice underneath.

If you steady the wood with one hand you can tilt it or turn it to meet the edge of the tool.

The wedge of scrap wood is a help when you want to work along the bottom edge. Work systematically down, with the grain or obliquely across it.

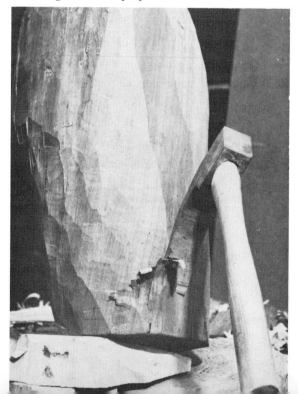

Visualise the basic shape of your idea inside the wood you are working on. Remove the unwanted wood in wide planes, thinking to yourself, 'This is what I want the basic shape to be. I must get rid of this waste wood here, then that bit there.'

Turn the work round and round so that you do not carve any one area for too long at a time, at the expense of the shape as a whole.

If the tool keeps digging into the wood, splitting the wood away more deeply than you want, you are cutting against the grain. Turn the wood the other way round (or the other way up) and work in the opposite direction. You will then be cutting with the grain. The carved surface will be smooth and controlled.

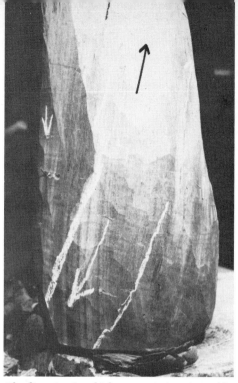

The direction in which you carve is governed by the grain of the wood. The arrows show the direction in which I carved this piece of wood.

This is the wood you are working on.

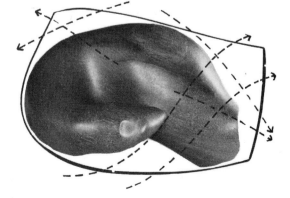

This is how you should be thinking.

CARVING WITH A GOUGE
AND MALLET

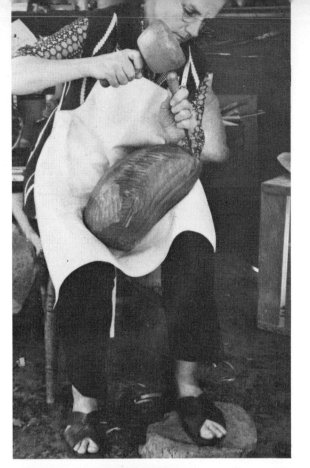

Your wood is now as near to the basic shape of your original idea as you can make it with an adze or an axe.

If you plan a finished shape with concave surfaces, with more complicated surface movements and with greater detail, you will need to start using a gouge and mallet.

If the wood is light enough you can place it in your lap. The leather apron will hold it and a pad of sacking or corduroy will protect the apron, should the tool slip.

Put one foot on a block or on the slice of end-grain wood. This will raise one side of the lap to steady the carving and will make a pad to work against.

Position your thumb along the gouge handle to guide the tool accurately in the right direction. It will also help to maintain an even depth of cut. Carve parallel channels of even depth along the grain or obliquely across it. Think always just ahead of the cutting edge of the gouge and plan systematically to cut away the waste wood, leaving a controlled surface.

If the tool splits the wood away, you are carving against the grain. Turn the wood round and carve in the opposite direction. Your gouge marks should then be smooth, even channels over the whole area.

Hold your wrist down on to the wood to steady it . . .

. . . or steady the carving against the edge of the bench.

36

(Right) If the wood is a large piece, you will want to work on the bench, placing the wood against the angled 'stop' which you have nailed to the bench or table top (p 16).

Adjust the work so that you are always hitting towards the 'stop'. If the wood is unsteady, use a wedge of scrap wood to level it or hold your wrist against the carving as you work.

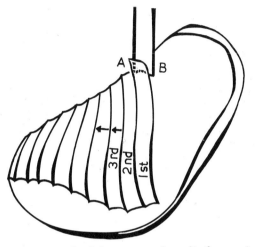

A splits the wood while B stops the split from going further into the wood than you want. The result will be a clean, controlled surface.

The corner A of the gouge is cutting into the wood, while corner B is out of the wood. When that channel is completed, the next one will be one gouge-width over to the left of the picture and so on, across the area to be carved.

The arrows chalked on the wood are only for the purpose of these photographs, to show the directions in which the gouge must travel because of the grain.

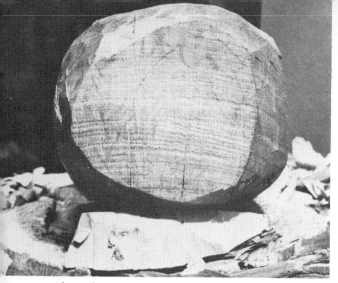

The end grain of a piece of wood is hard and brittle.

Be prepared to remove only a little wood at a time, using a narrower, deeper gouge than the one you used before. Be certain that your tool is really sharp. If the wood is very hard, choose a tool with a narrow bevel.

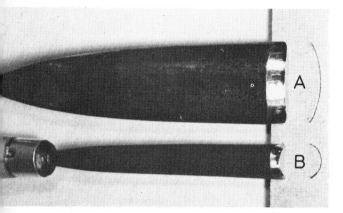

A is for soft wood and for carving along the grain.

B is for hard wood and for carving the end grain.

It is most important that your gouge cuts should be an even depth.

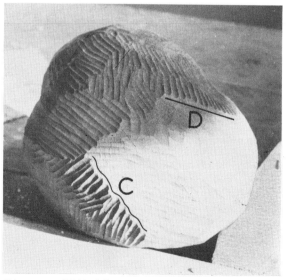

C is wrong. D is right.

Decide upon the area of wood that you wish to remove.

Carve parallel channels along the growth rings if possible, or obliquely across them.

Be satisfied with small, narrow channels. If you cut too deeply, the wood will either break away in tufts, pulling out from under the tool and leaving a badly pitted surface, or it will not break away at all and you may break your tool.

If a piece of gouge does snap off inside the wood, do not immediately take another gouge into the same cut but clear the wood away very carefully with a smaller, shallower tool until you have removed the splinter of steel; otherwise this will break the next gouge that you use.

If you follow the method described on p 37, of leaving part of your gouge out to one side of the carved channel, moving systematically across the area to be carved, you will find that the wood splits away evenly, leaving a tidy, controlled surface.

Work nearer and nearer to the final shape, turning the work over and round, carving evenly on all surfaces.

THINKING TOWARDS
GREATER DETAIL

You have completed the basic shape of your idea. The main proportions, the height, depth and length are to your liking. The surface movements are well defined and the surface itself is controlled.

Only when the basic shape of your work is completely established, should you think of carving any nearer to the detailed finish of your idea.

Work systematically, thinking of the direction, and the change of direction, of the planes on the surface.

Ideally they should change continually in all three dimensions but the rates of change should vary, contrasting and balancing one against another.

Think always of the positive surface, the surface that you want, and how it will affect the shape of your idea as a whole.

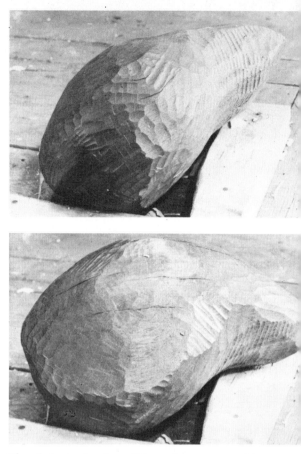

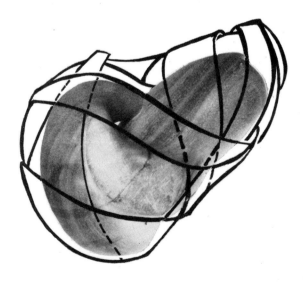

The photographs show the wood you are working on.

The drawing shows how you should be thinking.

HOLLOWS

As these contrasts become sharper you will need to follow the planes of movement by cutting 'valleys' into the depth of the wood.

(Right) Use a deeper gouge. Cut obliquely along the grain, starting each channel on the surface that you want, but cutting down into the waste wood that you do not want. Stop each channel in the centre of the 'valley' leaving the loose ends of the shavings still in the wood.

Turn the work round and cut towards the line of channels you have carved, meeting the other shavings in a line down the middle of the 'valley'.

(Below) These shavings will provide a buffer, preventing the tool from slipping into the opposite side of the hollow.

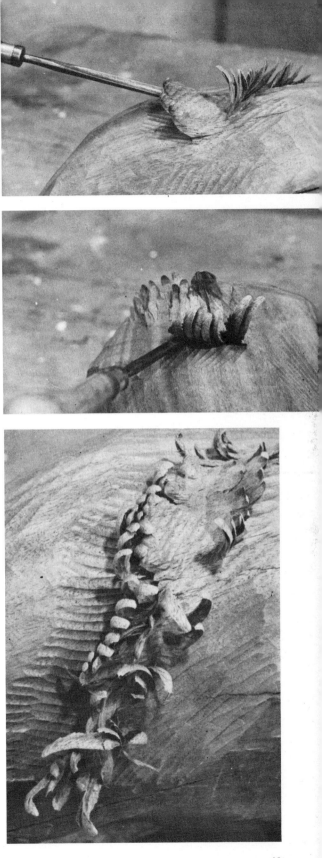

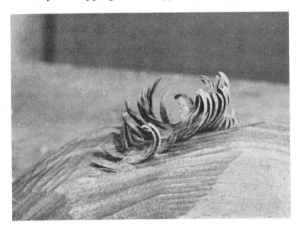

CUTTING A HOLE

As the 'valleys' become deeper and the detail of your work comes nearer to the finished idea, you may want to cut right through the wood.

It is easy to spoil a planned shape by using a drill to start a hole. The danger is that, being so straight, it will cut through, not as part of the design, but in spite of it, and you will not be able to shape the result to your liking.

Carve along the surfaces that you want, cutting spirally towards the centre of the waste wood on both sides of the work, leaving the shavings in the centre as a buffer. The position and direction of the hole will then be part of the design, as will the shape of the hole itself.

1

2 *3*

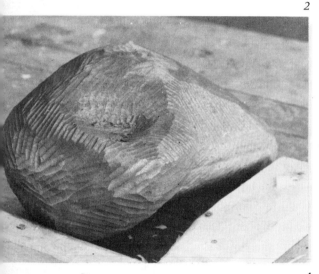

4 *5*

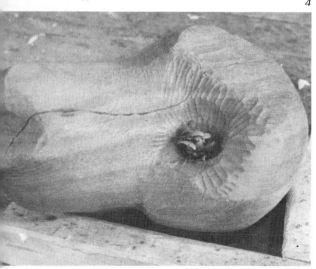

Visualise the hole, its shape, where it will begin and where it will come through to the outer side of the work. Remember to check that the grain of the wood lies along, and not across, any thin part of your design.

Cut toward the centre of the hole and stop each cut there, leaving the shavings in the centre to prevent the gouge from slipping into the opposite surface.

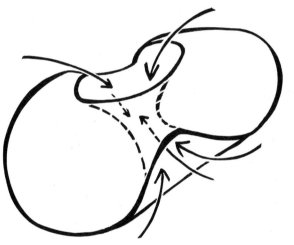

Work at the hole from both sides of the carving at once, thinking always of the positive, wanted surface and its relationship to the design as a whole.

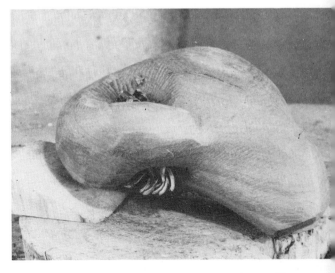

The beginning of the hole on one side of the work   *The beginning of the hole on the other side of the work*

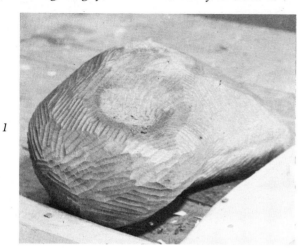

1

1

2

2

3

3

1

2

2

3

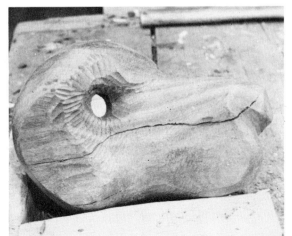

3

USING A SURFORM FILE

Use a Surform file at this stage of the work, to level the small channel edges left by the gouge.

Because of the action required in pushing it obliquely along the grain of the wood, it will accentuate the changing surface movements which you have developed as you carved with the gouge.

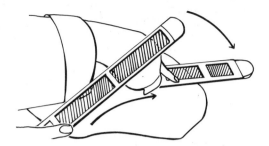

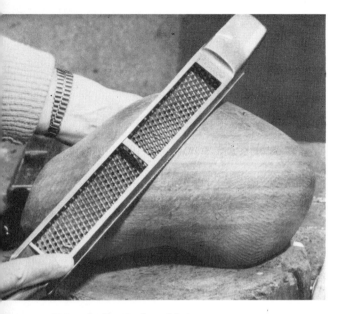

Using the flat Surform blade . . .

. . . push it forward and sideways in the same movement.

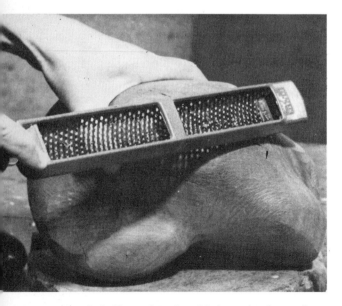

Using the half-round Surform blade, push it forward and sideways and . . .

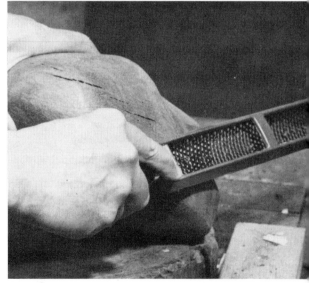

. . . at the same time, turn the tool to follow the curve of the carving.

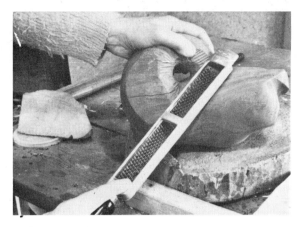

Pushing the tool forward and sideways . . .

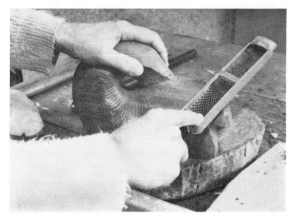

. . . you can also turn the work, if it is light enough, to meet the cutting face of the blade.

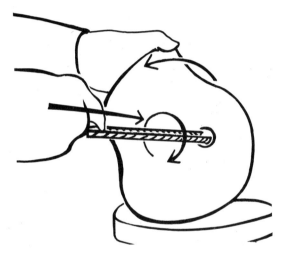

With the round Surform you can twist the blade and turn the work . . .

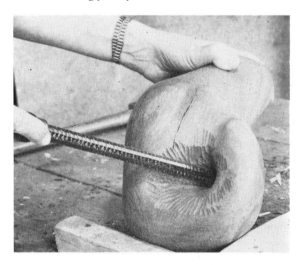

. . . finishing the shape of the hole that you began with the gouge.

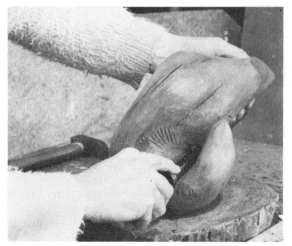

FINISHING THE CARVING

You have carved your piece of wood to the shape of your original idea, reviewing critically the design as a whole and altering it, as you carved, to suit the character of the particular piece of wood you chose.

Before you can carve more elaborate details if you want them, you must decide on the type of finished surface which you prefer.

The scale of detail, if it is to have any value as part of the shape of your sculpture, must depend on the final surface. It is no use working on a delicately carved eyelid if the cheek beside it is roughly gouged or scored with deep scratches.

What matters is the shape and how it feels to the hand or to the mind's hand. The choice is between the purist's tooled surface and the smooth polished finish.

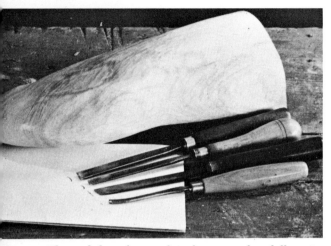

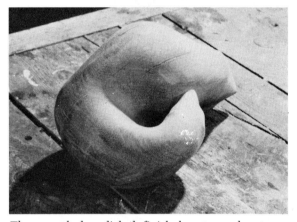

The tooled surface makes the most of a dull grain. The facets of the tooling catch the light, making the uninteresting material seem more alive.

The smoothed, polished finish has two advantages. The action of rubbing the surface ensures the flowing movement from one area of the carving to another and enhances the natural line of the grain.

The carving then seems not to have been worked by hand, but to have grown into shape as part of the tree.

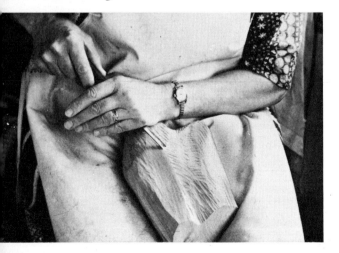

EBONY *Dancer*

BERMUDA CEDAR *Squirrel*

JARRAH *Squirrel*

ROSEWOOD *Snake*

The process of finishing with the tool is described in the section on p 78. I will continue the shape that we have been carving by smoothing and polishing the final surface, which is the finish that I think is most suitable for this piece of wood and for my original idea.

The photographs show the surface of the carving after using the Surform file. There are still a few areas where the gouge channels have not been removed. You can clear these away with a shallow gouge or a file. A half-round file will be particularly useful in the deep 'valleys'.

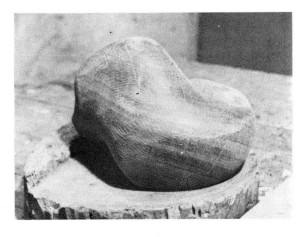

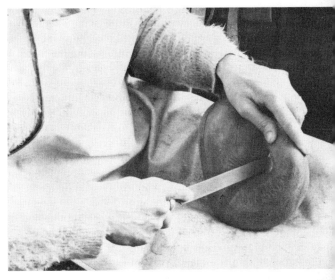

(Above) Move the file obliquely along the grain as you used the Surform blades but be careful not to file against the grain or you will seriously damage the final wood surface.

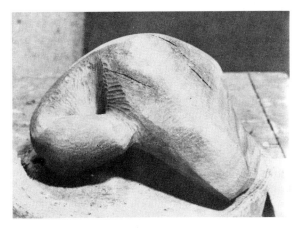

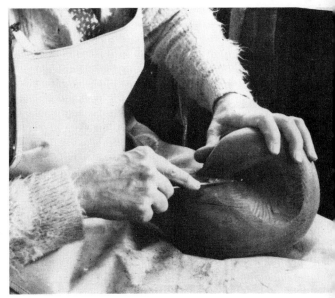

(Above) A riffler is another useful tool for clearing away the waste wood in any sharp curves and corners.

ABRASIVE CLOTH STRIP

The principle behind the process of the smooth, polished finish is, of course, that the surface of the carving is rubbed with progressively finer abrasives until all the tool marks have been removed. This leaves the wood surface completely unmarked, burnished and displaying the full depth of colour in the natural figure of the grain.

The advantage of using abrasive cloth strip is that you are not only refining the surface but you are, at the same time, perfecting the shape of the sculpture as a whole.

Cut about 18in of strip from the roll. Pull it diagonally across the carving as described in the photographs. Use it in the same way to clean out the inside of any holes in the work.

Be very careful not to let the strip wear a groove in the surface. If you are pulling it from end to end and are not allowing it to travel forwards and backwards at the same time, this is sure to happen and it will take a lot of time and patience to re-establish the wanted surface underneath once this mistake has been made.

There are coarse, medium and fine grades of the strip but you will find the medium is the most useful and it will practically finish the surface of your carving.

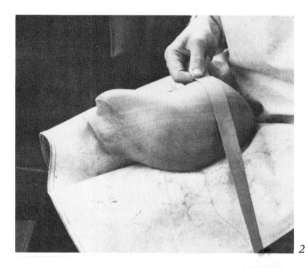

Move in one broad sweep, across from 1 through 4 and 5, and back again. Pull the strip from one end to the other and at the same time allow it to travel sideways over the surface movements of your design.

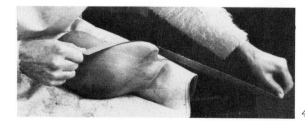

2

3

4

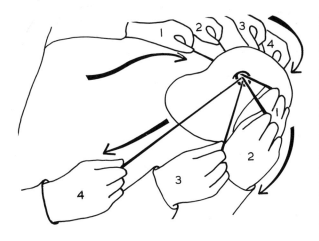

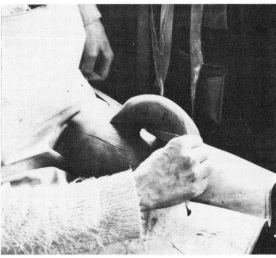

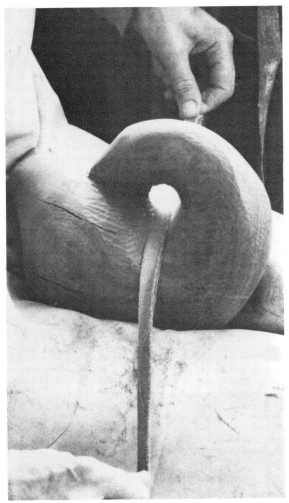

Thread the strip right through the hole, pulling the ends of the strip and keeping it stretched against the surface of the wood. The abrasive action will then run spirally through the hole.

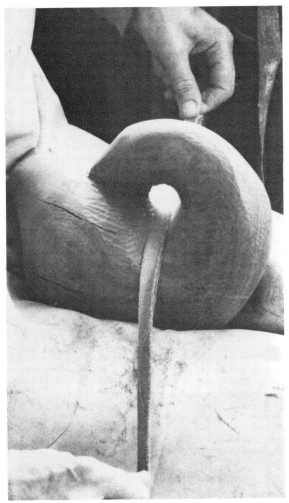

2

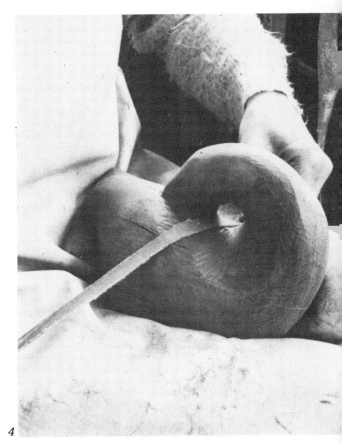

3

Tear the strip in half lengthwise if the holes or the curves are small.

4

PREPARING THE
FINAL SURFACE

Continue to rub down your carving until tool marks and scratches have disappeared using progressively finer 'wet and dry' paper. Using an old pair of scissors, cut off the amount of paper you need. Do not tear it or the loose edges will scratch your wood.

Use it dry but if it clogs up badly you can clean it under the tap and use it again when it has dried out.

It is a help to have a selection of grades of 'wet and dry' spaced approximately 100, 180, 240, 360, 480 and 600 grit, the last being used only after the surface is completely free of all other marks.

Many people will find it advisable to wear a dust mask when rubbing down most woods. Yew, teak and black bean are particularly irritant.

Damp the surface of the carving. This will bring the grain fibres up from the surface of the wood. Rub these down with 600 paper until the whole surface is quite smooth again. Repeat the wetting, drying and rubbing until there are no loose fibres left and the carving is smooth even when it is damp.

Collect some of the fine dust from this rubbing. You may need it to fill any cracks which have developed in your carving as you worked on it.

Some people feel that small cracks should not be filled, being part of the nature of the material, but I prefer to fill them, not so much to hide or to colour them, as to leave the surface unbroken and level to the touch.

If you are not sure that the wood was properly seasoned, leave it for a few weeks until the cracks no longer open and close in the changing weather conditions. When the wood is quite stable clean out the cracks with a brush or with the blower end of a vacuum cleaner.

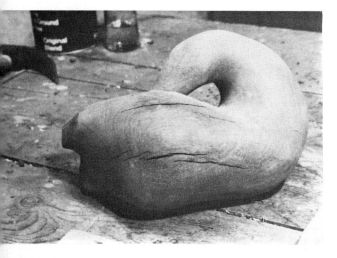

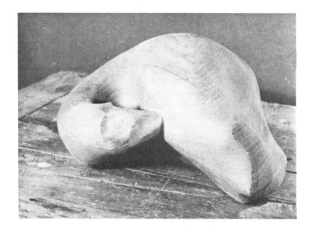

There are several methods of filling these cracks.

One is to use a standard make of 'plastic wood'. Choose a colour similar to that of your wood and follow the instructions on the tube or tin. Press the paste firmly into the cracks leaving it proud of the wood surface. It will shrink as it hardens so that a series of applications should be made, allowing each layer to dry before adding more. When it is thoroughly dry, rub it down to the level of the wood surface with 'wet and dry' paper.

There is also a proprietary brand of 'stopper' which is water-soluble so that the unwanted stopper, along the sides of the cracks, can be wiped away with a damp cloth, before being rubbed down to the wood surface.

Or you can use a paste made from the fine dust (collected when rubbing down the carving) with one of the synthetic glues.

There are two types of this glue. One, especially made for using on wood, is supplied as a powder, which you mix with water, then add the wood dust from your carving, and finally mix in the hardener or drip it into the cracks after you have filled them with the paste. (If you are using this on oak, you must not allow the hardener to come into contact with any metal or it will stain the wood black.)

Because this glue can be absorbed by the wood fibres, which makes it so good for normal glueing-up operations, there is a slight shrinkage in this filling and it has a tendency to stain the sides of the cracks.

The other type of synthetic glue is supplied in two tubes: one of resin, the other of hardener.

Measure and mix these according to the instructions on the tubes; add the wood dust; then force the paste into the cracks with a thin sliver of wood. Leave the filling proud of the wood.

When the glue is hard, after about three days at normal room temperature, file away the unwanted filling, using the file brush to clean the file, then smooth the surface with 'wet and dry' paper. I find this last method to be the most satisfactory. It is easier to mix accurately and there is no shrinkage at all. The colour may be a little dark when it is finished, but the surface is hard and smooth to the touch.

The best method of all for filling small cracks, particularly in hard wood, is that of using shellac on a hot knife, as described on p 64.

Now that you have filled the cracks in your carving, the surface is ready to be polished, but you must first consider whether you wish to mount it.

Various types of mounts are described on p 82, but I think that for this particular carving, which is a shape in space not only to be looked at but to be handled, it would spoil it to fix it in any way.

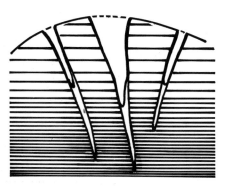

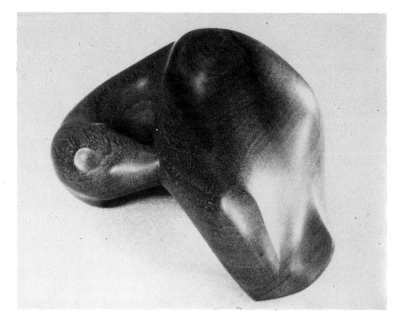

If your carving does not stand at quite the angle that you would like, follow the process, described on p 70, of altering the angle of the base.

(Right) Make the carving stand level by flattening the areas underneath with a Surform file and sliding the work to and fro on a sheet of medium 'wet and dry' paper which has been fixed to a flat surface. Avoid getting any polish on to these flattened areas to which you will glue some felt when the carving is finished.

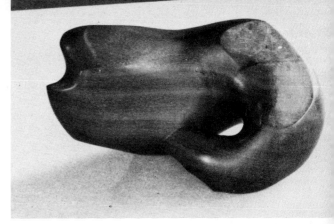

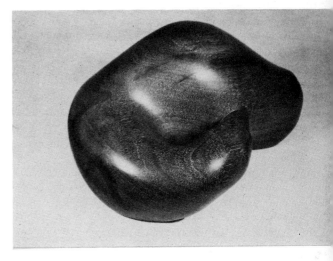

1 *Apply one coat of silicone wax polish to your carving, rubbing it well into the wood. Rub over the whole surface with a clean, soft cloth.*

3

With a small piece of worn 600 grit 'wet and dry' paper, rub over the waxed surface, first gently, then with increasing pressure until the carving is burnished all over. 2

4

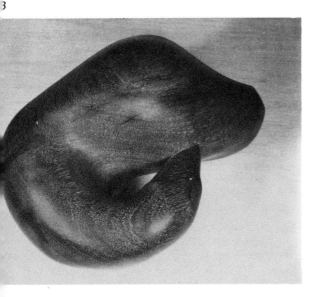

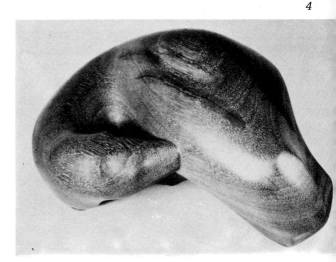

1

Spread some glue (Glue-all or Uhu are suitable) on to the flat areas underneath.

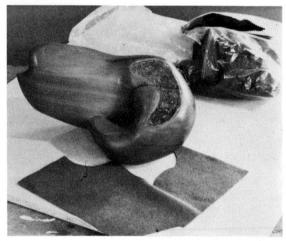

2

Choose some felt to match the wood and place it over the glued areas.

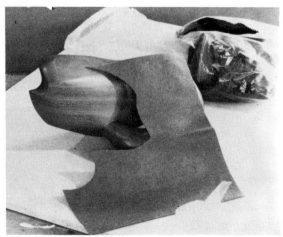

3

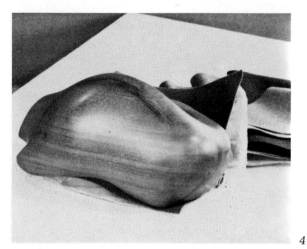

4

Stand the carving the right way up on the felt on a clean flat surface so that its own weight will hold the felt in place while the glue dries.

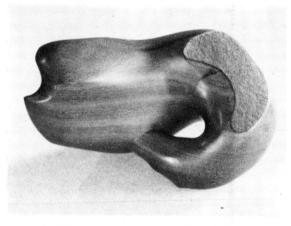

5

Trim the felt with scissors, a very sharp knife or a razor blade, taking care not to mark the wood.

Give your carving a final polish with a soft cloth.

Now that it is finished, how does the final shape compare with the original idea?

Does it convey in essence, the character of the original subject?

Do the surface movements carry your hand (or your mind's hand) from one part of the shape to another, over the whole piece of sculpture?

Do you think that your carving looks as though it had been skilfully made, but in spite of the material; or does it look, as it should, as if it had grown that way?

These are the questions that you should ask yourself when you are criticising your own work. I hope that you are pleased with it.

THE SECOND METHOD OF WORKING

This is the carving for which you have no planned shape in your imagination. Until now you have been visualising the finished carving inside the wood as you worked on it. You have developed the character of your idea within the material. You may prefer to choose a piece of wood for its own shape; to carve it until you have developed its natural qualities to your liking, without necessarily attaching an illustrative idea to the finished work.

Examine the wood from every angle so that you can really appreciate its shape.

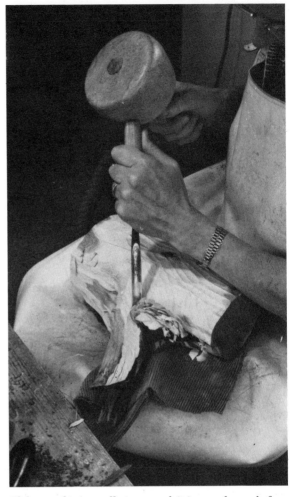

If the wood is a small piece, work it in your lap as before. Remove the bark and the sapwood. Remove the split ends of the branches.

The direction of the grain will change around the knots where the branches join the main stem. Clear away the hard wood round the knots with a small gouge, working very gently. The arrows drawn on the wood show the direction of the gouge cuts.

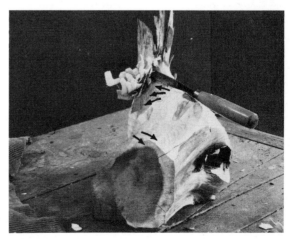

The practical technique of this carving is exactly the same as that of the previous one but the thinking is entirely different.

Before, you were concerned with a trinity: the idea, the shape and the material. Now you are interested in only two problems: developing a good shape within the character of the material.

When you have removed the sapwood, the split ends of the branches and any areas of dead wood, turn the piece of wood about on the bench or in your hand, so that you really appreciate its natural shape, colour and character.

Plan to remove wood where you feel that the shape 3 needs defining. Develop the natural surface movements to improve the shape as a whole. Use a wide shallow gouge to cut away the wood from the main stem.

4

1

2

Use a small deep gouge to clear out the hollows above the branches.

5

It would be interesting to develop these hollows.

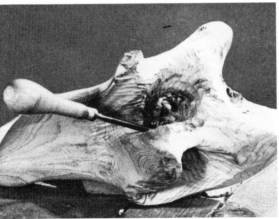

1

Is the wood strong enough for you to carve right through?

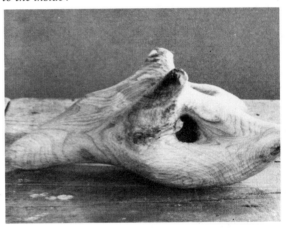

4

Where does the natural movement lead from the outside to the inside?

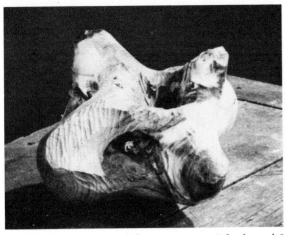

2

What shape is 'growing' between these hollows?

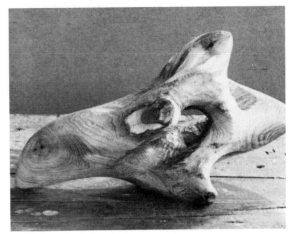

5

Use the Surform file to reduce the gouge marks.

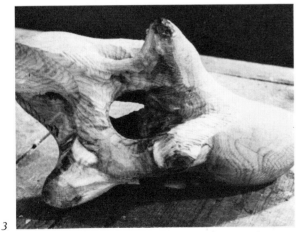

3

If you go through one, will it be a good shape if you go through another? What shape will develop between the two?

6

The riffler and file will clear out the inside.

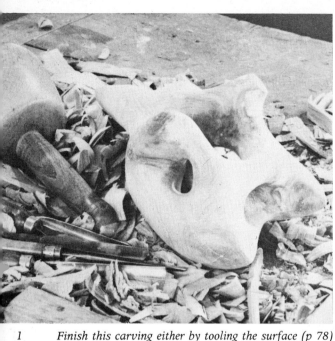

1   *Finish this carving either by tooling the surface (p 78) or with fine abrasives as you did the last one.*

Wear a mask when rubbing down yew, teak, or black bean.

2

3   *If there is a hole in the centre of the heartwood, or any area that needs repair, it may be best to patch it with a piece of the same wood.*

Cut a piece of wood larger than the hole you are filling, but matching in colour, and with the grain, as far as possible, similar to that around the hole. Shape this to a cone or pyramid shape with the base larger than the hole, the tip smaller and the height less than the depth of the hole.   4

Place the base of this cone centrally over the hole and draw round it on your wood. Clean up the edges of the hole keeping well within the pencil marks, leaving the inside of the hole bevelled, where possible, at an angle slightly steeper than that of the cone.

Apply some synthetic glue to the inside surfaces of the hole and to the cone then press the cone into the hole, tapping it gently into place.

Bandage it with an adhesive tape to hold it firmly until the glue is thoroughly dry.

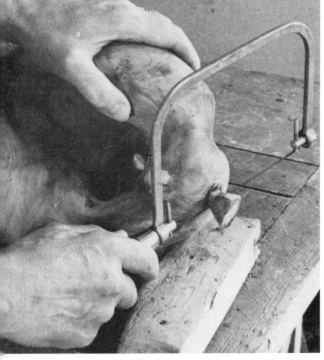

Saw off the waste wood.

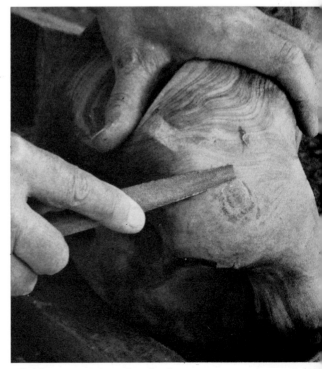

File the remaining surface level.

63

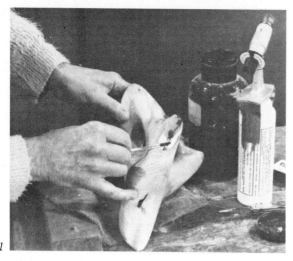

1

The most likely cracks in this type of wood are the tiny hair-cracks in the dark heartwood. The best way to fill these is with shellac.

Put some flakes of shellac into a tin lid. Heat the end of an old knife blade in a clean flame: use a gas or methylated spirit flame, rather than a candle flame.

Dip the hot knife into the shellac, lifting a flake or two from the tin.

Press the shellac, as it melts on the knife, into the crack.

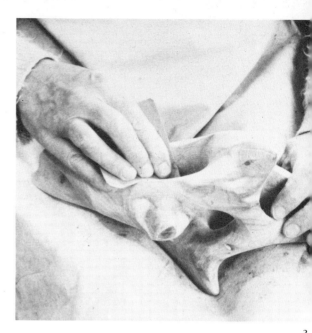

3

Use finer grades of 'wet and dry' paper until all tool marks have disappeared. Wet the surface of the carving, rub down with 600 grit paper when dry. Repeat until the grain ceases to rise.

2

It will harden as it cools and can be polished to match the surrounding wood.

4

This is the stage at which to use water-soluble stopper, if you like to, in any small surface cracks that are still showing. Wipe away the surplus stopper with a damp cloth.

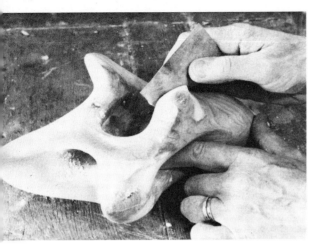

Give the carving a final rub with 600 'wet and dry' paper, used dry. Apply one coat of silicone wax polish, rub with a soft cloth and burnish with a small piece of worn, very fine, 'wet and dry' paper.

It is well worth using a silicone wax polish on a carving that is going to be handled. The 'antique' type, or ordinary wax polishes show the finger marks at once.

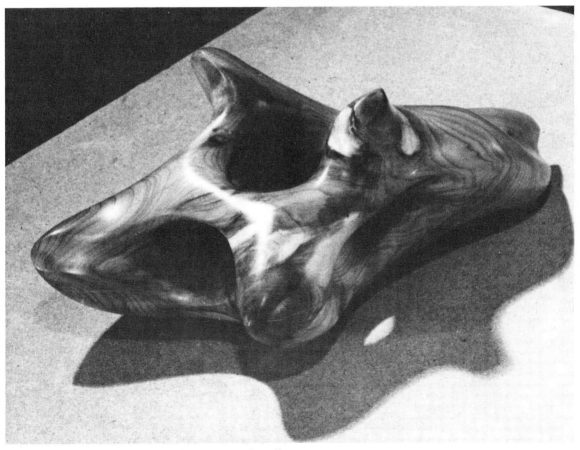

This carving is meant to be handled. I hope people will enjoy it for its shape as well as for the amazing colours in the grain of the wood.

CARVING A HEAD

Because some people regard the portrait head as a specialised field of sculpture, the following photographs show a small head in the making.

The techniques are the same as those used in the earlier carvings but there are several points worth noting.

Visualise the basic shape of the finished work as a whole.

Cut a piece of wood large enough to allow plenty of extra material. Do not underestimate the distances from the back of the head to the front of the nose or chin.

Choose a wood without too much contrast in the grain. If you place the features centrally, in line with the layers of the annual rings, the contrasts in the grain may conflict with the features in the carving resulting in an unfortunate coincidence of markings.

(Below) Be careful to choose the best direction for the grain of the wood, which will tend to split from the centre of the heartwood outwards.

2

3

(Below) Position the features so that any likely splits will occur away from the face and not down the centre of the thinnest parts, as, for instance, down the length of the nose.

1

4

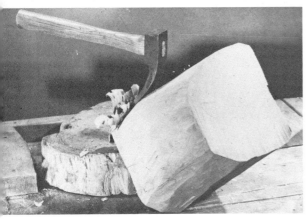

Establish the basic shape, first with the adze and then with the gouge.

Clear away the gouge cuts with a Surform file, stressing the surface movements from one part of the design to another.

4

5

6

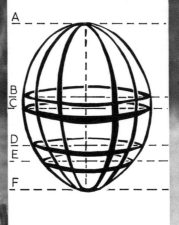

These lines may help you to plan the proportions of the face.

The head is basically the shape of an egg on an axis which measures from the top of the scalp A, to the point of the chin F. It is interesting to note that the eyes are on the line C which is halfway down the line A-F.

The nose rests on a line D halfway between the line of the brow B and the chin F. The mouth is on a line E, one-third of the distance between D and F.

The ears rest between the lines B and D and on the sketch of the plan view you can see how their shape begins to leave the head a quarter of the way round the circumference from the centre of the brow. These proportions may be only slightly different for every face. The real subtlety of likeness and 'aliveness' will be in the spiral movements of the surface planes.

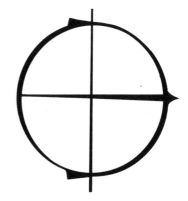

Work out the area of the features in terms of these movements and their relation to the shape as a whole. Think of your tool peeling them off, like onion layers, as you work nearer and nearer to the finished surface. (The carved head is not a portrait of the girl in the pictures above.)

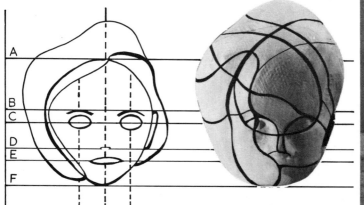

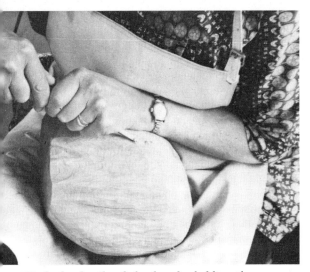

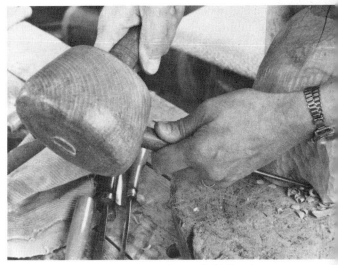

1 Work the details of the face by holding the gouge or chisel in the hand. With one hand holding the tool, pushing it forward into the wood, the other hand steadies it, helps to direct it and prevents it from slipping.

Wedge the work between your lap and the bench. You 4 can carve into the slice of end-grain wood as before.

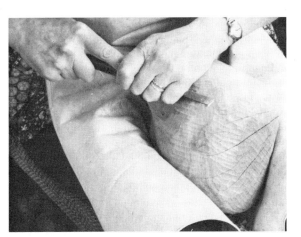

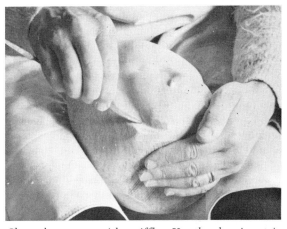

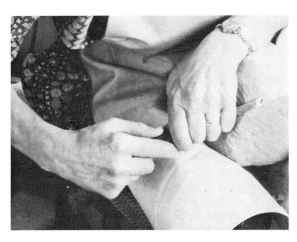

Clean the corners with a riffler. Use the abrasive strip to stress and simplify the surface movements as well as to smooth away the tool marks.

2

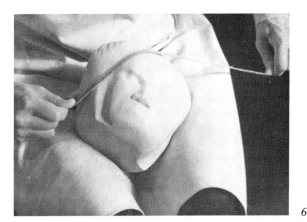

3

5

6

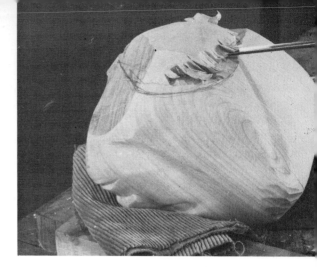

ALTERING THE BASE

I think the shape of this head is too square. If it were tilted a little, showing the roundness underneath, it would be more interesting to look at. This is one of the only two occasions when you should draw on the surface of your carving. The other is when you are patching a damaged piece of wood.

Hold the head in the position in which you think it looks best. Prop it up with a wedge of scrap wood. Hold a pencil on, or against, another piece of wood and move it round the carving so that the pencil draws a line parallel to the bench or table top.

Draw firmly all the way round the carving however strange the angle may seem to be at the time.

You can now remove the unwanted wood along the line, or parallel to it, either with a saw or by cutting it away tidily with a shallow gouge.

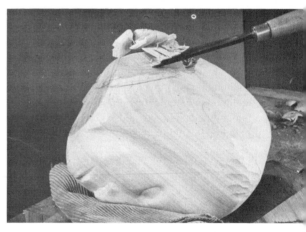

1

To finish the levelling process, if there is a lot of un-evenness, stand the carving on a piece of carbon paper, on a flat surface. Move the carving gently from side to side until the carving is marked on the underside where it touches the carbon. This will show you where the 'high spots' are.

2

Remove these with a Surform or file, and repeat until the carving stands absolutely level.

3

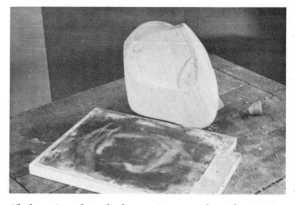

4

If there is only a little unevenness, place the carving directly on a sheet of abrasive paper which has been fixed to a flat surface. Moving the carving to and fro a few times will rub off any roughness and the carving will stand firm.

5

Continue to rub down the rest of the carving with 'wet and dry' paper, wetting the surface as before, until the grain will not rise any more.

'LIFTS' IN THE GRAIN

Sometimes, when the area which you are carving is at a very shallow angle to the natural layers of the grain, the edges of these layers will lift up slightly. Any attempt to rub down this 'lift' with abrasives rubs the dust in, under the edge of the layer, lifting it still further. You may avoid this by rubbing in one direction only, from the centre of the lifting area outwards; or you can scrape down the surface (scraping away from the centre) with the edge of a piece of freshly broken glass.

This should be rolled glass, not cast glass. The latter breaks with a jagged edge, the former with a smooth sharp edge, though the initial sharpness will wear off quite quickly, even without use.

1   *Put a piece of rolled glass (picture glass is good) into a paper bag on a flat surface.*

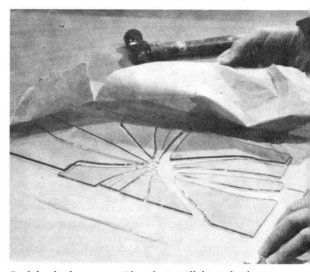

Peel back the paper. The glass will have broken into clean, slightly curved wedges.

One side of the edge may be sharper than the other. Use the sharpest edge to scrape the surface of your carving, working from the centre of the lifting area outwards.

2   *Give it one sharp tap with a hammer, just hard enough to break the glass with the one blow.*

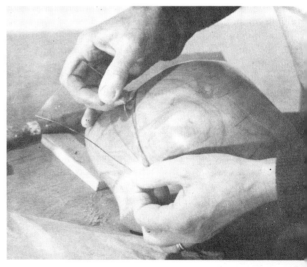

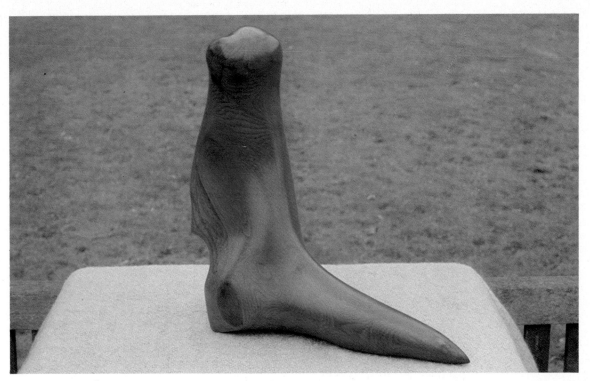

YEW *Otter, standing*

WALNUT *Pigeon*

MAHOGANY *Girl with Plaits*

TEAK *Cat, hunting*

1

Fill the cracks with stopper or, if you kept some of the dust from the rubbing, mix it with a synthetic glue to make a paste. Force this into the cracks with a thin sliver of wood. Leave it proud of the surface and allow to dry.

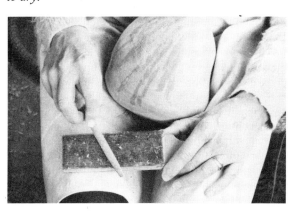

2

Remove the surplus filler with a file which you can clean with a file brush.

3

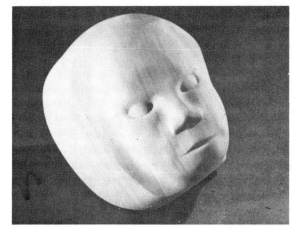

4

Finish the carving with silicone wax polish, rubbed with a soft cloth and then burnished with a small piece of waxed 600 grit 'wet and dry' paper. Glue a suitable coloured felt on to the bottom of the carving and trim the edges.

6

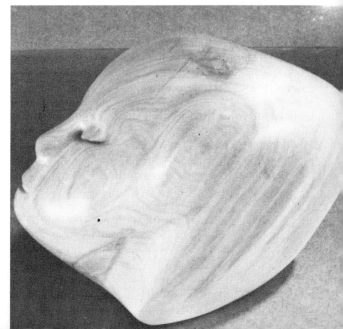

MAKING A 'GROUP' MOBILE

The popular idea of a mobile is a group of shapes, hanging or fixed, free to turn about each other in a three-dimensional pattern.

Because of the quality of weight in wood, and the pleasure in the feel of it, I think it is a mistake to fix it rigidly in any way at all.

Shapes that hang balanced to turn in space, cannot be handled and though it may be interesting to make one of these in a very lightweight wood, I find the 'group' form of mobile much more suited to the material.

The important thing in this case is, of course, the proportion of the pieces that make up the group and the interchange of rhythmic surface movements between them. If the units are from the same piece of wood, they will blend in colour and in character; while the careful use of the grain should complement the relationship between them.

Ideally, the design as a whole should never seem to be at rest but should always be inviting a re-arrangement of the units so that the group, because of its shape, is truly a mobile.

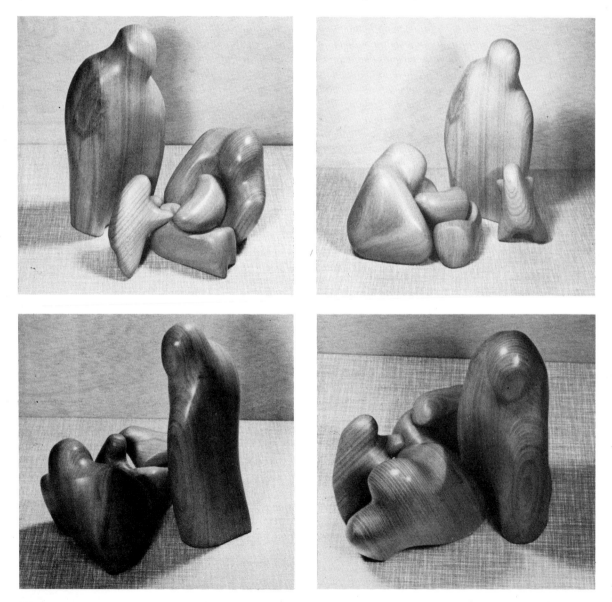

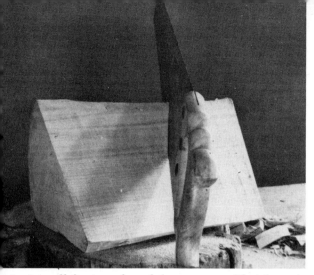

1   *Saw off the sizes of wood that you want. Plan the grain as you cut the pieces.*

Value one shape against another and the size of each in proportion to the whole.   2

3

4

Try to see the finished work in your mind. Where before you were concerned with the surface movements of one piece of sculpture, here these same rhythms must travel to and fro, blending and contrasting, between the different shapes of the group.

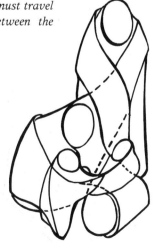

5

THE SMALL FIGURES
FOR THE MOBILE

I would shape pieces as small as this mainly by rubbing.

Saw off the size of wood that you want, then shape it with the adze, placing the slice of end-grain wood in your lap and holding the work firmly against it. This way you can turn the work round as you carve it, making sure that the basic shape is a good shape in all three dimensions.

Then use a Surform file, covering the hand that holds the wood with a piece of corduroy or canvas in case the Surform slips, particularly on the end-grain.

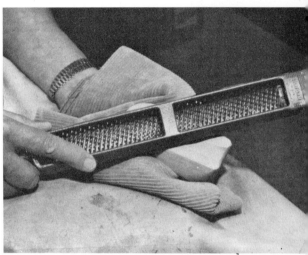

If the shape is well established in your own mind, and if you have an electric drill and a vice, you could use them here. Fix the drill in the vice, leaving the ventilation holes unobstructed.

Put an abrasive disc and rubber backing in the chuck. Hold the work against the disc. It is imperative that you should place yourself in such a position that you present the work to the downward turning surface of the disc, otherwise the dust, and indeed the work itself will be thrown upwards into your face. Keep the face out of line with the disc.

Steady the hand that holds the work either against your knee, if you are seated, or against the bench or table edge. Keep the work moving and only press gently or the wood will burn and the surface be too badly damaged to finish well.

Fit finer abrasive discs as you need them, or finish the work by hand once the shape is established to your liking.

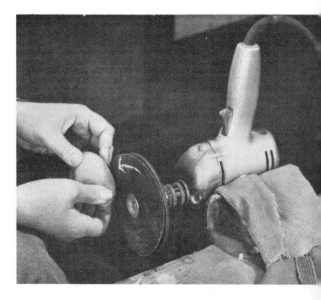

If you plan to saw a little off the base, hold it with the 'bench holdfast', carefully padding your carving wherever the grip might damage the surface.

2

1

Keep all the units of the group at the same level of development, so that you can study each shape as part of the whole. For instance, the upright figure of this family of shapes seems too tall when compared with the others.

At this stage you must decide on the finish. As these figures are small and have been shaped mostly by rubbing, I would think it best to give them a smooth finish, using 'wet and dry' paper to remove all the tool marks, and polishing with silicone wax polish.

3

4

A TOOLED SURFACE

Perhaps you would prefer to do the whole process of carving without using a file or abrasives of any kind.

This is a good method to use when the sculpture is very large or when the material lacks variety.

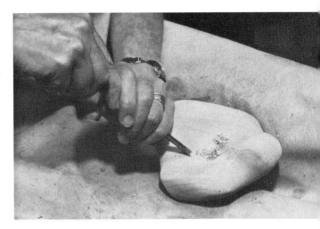

Hold the work against the angled 'stop' on the bench or, if it is light enough, carve it in the leather apron on your lap.

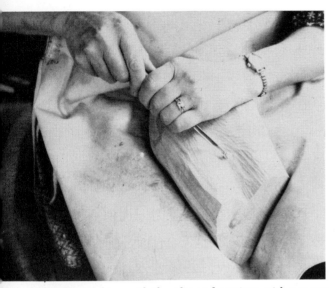

Begin working with the adze and continue with a gouge as before, but as you carve nearer to the finished surface, use a shallow gouge or a chisel without using the mallet.

Ease the tool forward with one hand and steady it with the other, pressing on it to guide it and to prevent it from slipping.

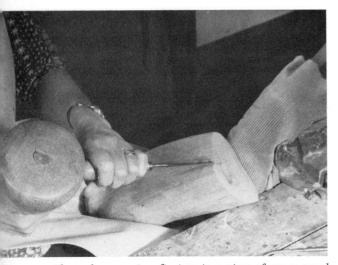

If you have a vice, fix into it a piece of scrap wood round which you have bound some padding, some

sacking or corduroy. This will make a useful buffer to work against.

These are the tools used on a small carving. A large sculpture could be finished with wide, flat chisels, and shallow gouges. Where the shapes are simple and the curved surfaces are convex, the adze alone would be sufficient.

When the carving is finished, regular facets of an even depth, like those on the planished surface of beaten copper, should be just discernible over the whole carving.

When these are polished with a wax polish, they will reflect the light, adding vitality to large areas of wood which might otherwise look rather monotonous.

One of the three 7ft-high figures by John Skeaping, commissioned by King's College, Cambridge, and now on loan to Lincoln Cathedral. Photographed by permission of the Dean of Lincoln Cathedral, and of King's College, Cambridge.

This photograph shows the tooled surface which is an ideal finish for such a large sculpture.

MOUNTING

Your piece of sculpture is a satisfactory design in all three dimensions. Ideally it is the perfect shape in space. The very completeness of it requires a compromise between the shape itself and the ground that it stands on.

The more rounded it is, the more separate it will be from its surroundings. For it to stand on its own, it must have a minimum of three points touching the ground, evenly spaced about the centre of gravity. The further apart these points can be, the more stable will be the result.

There will still be some shapes that need to be fixed to a separate base – usually those with a subject implying action, like running, swimming or flying. Then there is the perpetual problem of 'long thin legs', which is a matter of designing for the material.

The subject may be balanced on thin supports, but to design a shape which is suitable for a rigid, heavy material, these supports must be considered as part of the shape as a whole and they should either be incorporated in it, or, if they are not necessary to the design, ignored.

All but one of the carvings described earlier in this book, have been completed in this way (the yew abstract had no flattened surfaces), and we have put felt on any flat areas underneath to protect the surfaces on which the carving might be placed (see p 56).

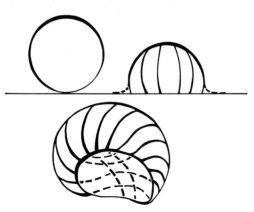

A rounded shape, cut off to a flat base becomes part of its horizon.

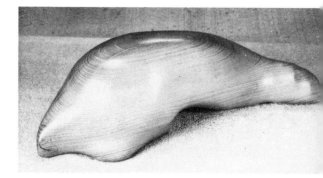

If you vary the angle at which the surface of the shape meets the horizon, the surface movements will carry the eye round the carving and through the base, implying a shape that is independent of the ground it stands on.

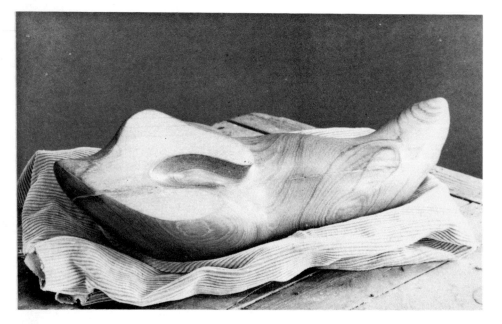

This carving needs a base or a mount. It is a small carving of a seagull made of satin-smooth boxwood. As its subject is a bird soaring, would you hang it from the ceiling? It might look attractive from underneath but on top it would require three fixing points for it to hang with any stability, so that even if you could reach it, you could not handle it in order to appreciate its shape or to enjoy the quality of the wood.

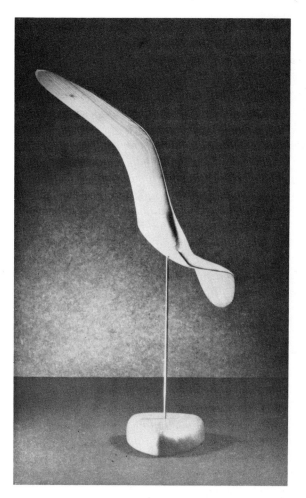

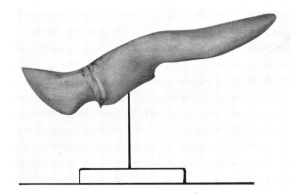

If you were to fix it on a stem, mounted on a base, you could at least turn it about and view it from all levels, but you still cannot handle it. The mount does not seem to suit the carving.

John Thorpe has mounted his soaring 'wing' in this way. For this particular carving the choice is ideal.

'Gull' by John Thorpe (ash)

Another idea is to mount your carving on a contrasting material.

The way Ken Wilkinson has mounted his 'Otter' and his 'Seal' is particularly suited to the subjects of these small carvings – indeed the otter and its rock are so much in keeping that the carving and its base are really two parts of the one whole shape.

Another possibility is a contrasting wooden base, either as part of the whole design, like George Taylor's 'Nuthatch' (below), or as a simple geometric shape, like his 'Thrush' (right), to support the weight and the height of works which might otherwise be unstable.

On the other hand the seal is fixed to its rock with minimum contact so that the shape stands free to express, in all three dimensions, the action of the swimming mammal. 2

The 'Thrush' was first mounted by a fairly long pin on to a rectangular base; but the wedge, with the bird fixed close to it, implies the same action without it looking 'one-legged'.

4

3

But our 'Seagull' does not look right on any of these mounts.

The great beauty of boxwood is in the feel of the close grain.

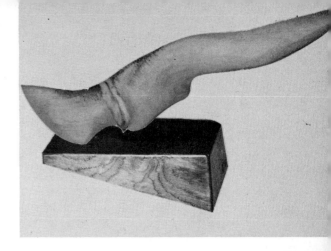

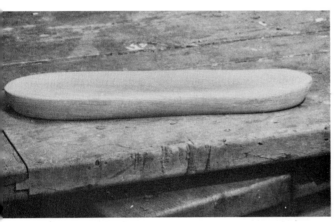

If we make a shallow saucer-shape out of a contrasting wood, the bird can be placed in it, poised there but held from falling.

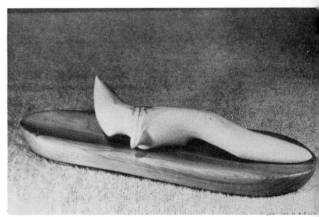

The underneath of this 'saucer' is covered with felt to protect the surfaces on which it will stand, so that the 'Seagull' can be handled and replaced with safety.

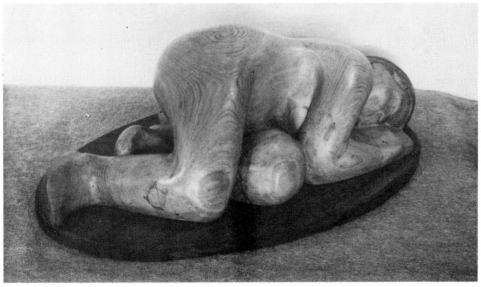

Thalia Polak has mounted her large carving on a wide shallow saucer-shape. It frames the carving beautifully.

'Sleeping Figure' by Thalia Polak (sweet chestnut)

The following photographs show a general method of fixing a carving to its base where the base is not rectangular either in elevation or in plan, and where the sculpture is too slim to risk drilling a hole for a screw or a pin, without careful marking.

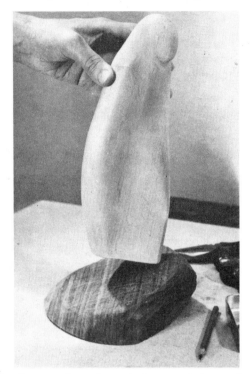

1

The first step is to shape the bottom of the carving so that it rests on the base at the correct angle.

Hold the carving against the base until you find the angle that suits it best.

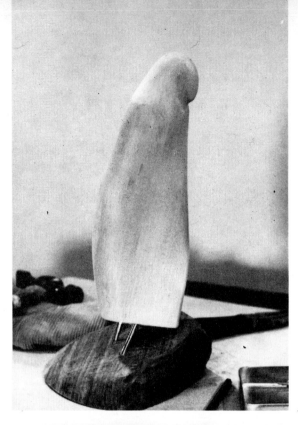

2

Drive two or more panel pins into the bottom of the carving. Tap them in gently until they are the right lengths to act as 'legs' on which the carving will balance at the correct angle, or anyway to act as a steady to help you to hold the carving in place while you mark round it.

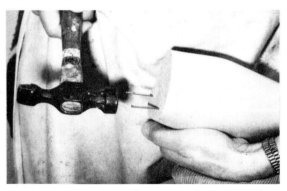

3

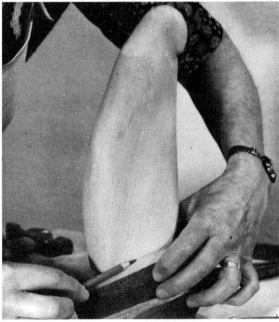

4

Rest a rectangular block of wood on the base against the carving. Draw a line on the carving, running the pencil along the level side of the block of wood moving all the way round the carving so that you have a firm line a little way up the carving, parallel to the proper angle of the base.

84

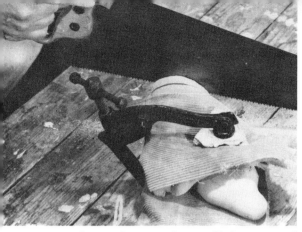

1 Remove the panel pins and saw off the unwanted wood. Wrap the carving with some padding and hold it on a block of scrap wood on the bench, fixing it firmly with the bench holdfast.

Saw along a line parallel to your pencil line, as near to the bottom of the carving as the angle of the line will allow.

2 Clean up the surface if necessary with a flat file, taking care not to round the flat area on the bottom by mistake.

2

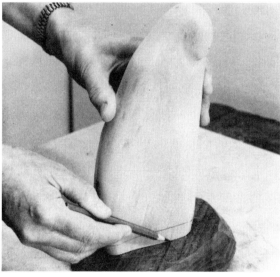

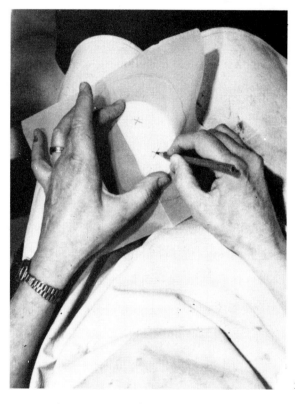

3 Hold the carving in its correct, final position on the base and draw round it.

4 Slip a piece of thin paper (tracing paper if possible) between the carving and the base and, still keeping the carving in exactly the right position, draw round it again on the paper.

5 Turn the carving and the paper with it, upside down on the bench or in your lap (above right). Mark on the paper the points where you can safely put screws into the work without damaging it. With a nail or a sharp point, make a small hole through the paper into the bottom of the carving to mark where these points come.

To be sure that you can locate the paper exactly, particularly if the base wood is dark, draw round the outer edge of the base itself, and write 'Top' on the paper to save any mistake later on (below left).

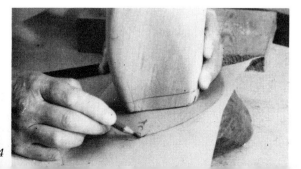

5

3

4

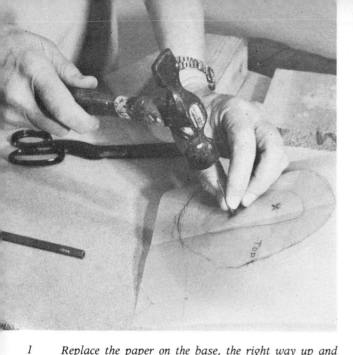

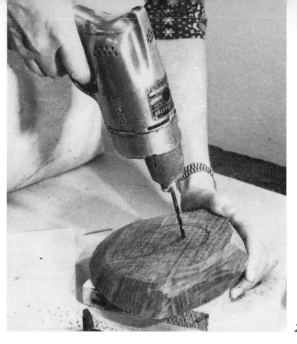

1   *Replace the paper on the base, the right way up and mark with a spike or nail, through the paper, the points where the screw holes should be made.*

    Choose the screw size from the chart on p 89. With the appropriate size of drill (for the thread, not for the shank) make holes into the base at the angle best suited to the carving but not straight into end grain. If someone else checks this angle for you it is easy, otherwise a mirror is useful placed first in front of you and then at the side to check the angle from both points of view.

So that you can drill right through the base, put a piece of soft scrap wood underneath it to protect the bench.

3   *To locate the carving on its base while you drill holes into it, tap two panel pins into the base within the pencilled area. Take them out again and cut the heads off with wire cutters or pliers. Tap them back into their holes, flat end in, point upwards.*

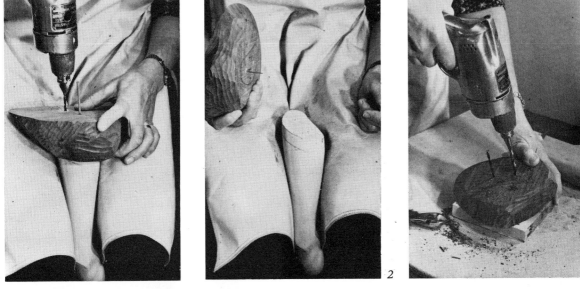

1

2

3

(Above left) Place the carving in the correct position on its base and press it down on to the sharp pins to keep it in that position. Hold the carving upside down on some padding on the bench or, if it is small enough, in the leather apron on your lap. Guided by the holes already drilled in the base and using the same-sized bit, drill down into the carving, measuring the depth of the hole for screw length.

(Above centre) Separate the carving from the base.

(Above right) With the shank-size drill, enlarge the holes in the base and countersink them well.

4

Work the screw gently into the carving to cut the thread. Remove the screw.

Clean up the edges of the holes, and then polish the base. Smear a little wax polish on to the screw thread to prevent rust.

Finally screw the base firmly on to the carving.

5

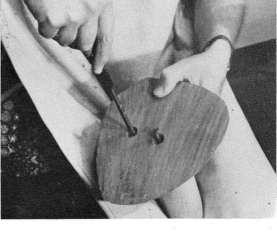

6

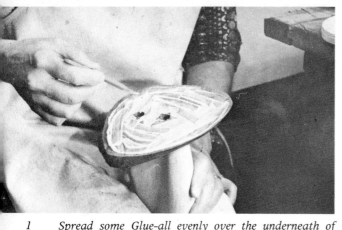

1   Spread some Glue-all evenly over the underneath of the base.

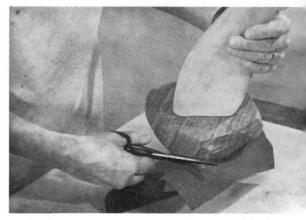

With sharp scissors, cut away the waste felt from around the edge of the base.

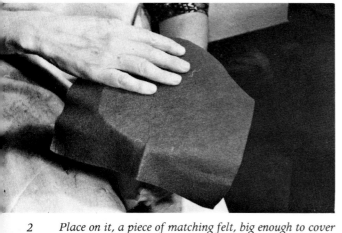

2   Place on it, a piece of matching felt, big enough to cover the whole area and press all over it with the flat of the hand.

Stand the mounted carving on the felt on a clean flat surface until the glue is dry.

If the base has a sharp edge, you can clean up the edge of the felt with a new, sharp file making a slight bevel outwards.

The mount is finished and your carving will stand firm.

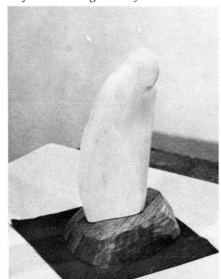

3

TIPS ON USING SCREWS

Many people have unnecessary difficulty when using screws.

If it is difficult, something is wrong. All ordinary wood screws are made to a standard formula:

The length (L) is stated in inches; the threaded part is about two-thirds L.

The diameter (D) of the shank is indicated by a gauge number; gauges 0–12 suit drills sizes going up from $\frac{1}{16}$ in to $\frac{1}{4}$ in by $\frac{1}{64}$ ths.

The diameter of the head is twice that of the shank, or 2D.

The diameter of the core of the thread is about half that of the shank, or $\frac{1}{2}$D.

Each screw requires two holes. The larger hole (through the base in the example) should just clear the shank of the screw. The smaller hole (into the carving) should match the size of the thread core. The countersinking should be slightly more than 2D, so that the head does not protrude.

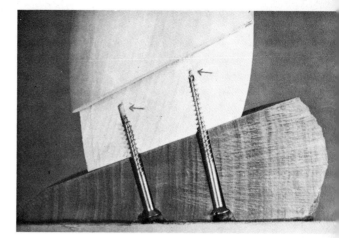

Section through mounted carving and base. Note: clearance in holes through base; spare depth in thread holes (arrowed); countersinking deep enough to prevent heads from protruding. The screws are at an angle to avoid screwing into end grain.

If difficulties arise, check that the shank fits easily in the clearance hole; further trouble means that the thread hole is too small, too short, or out of line.

Avoid, if possible, screwing straight into end grain; a small angle across the grain greatly increases holding power. Allow spare depth in thread hole; if the screw reaches the end too soon it tends to strip the wood thread from the hole. Cut a thread in the thread hole by working a screw in a little at a time (choose a well-cut screw) before final assembly; if this is difficult, enlarge the thread hole slightly. This reduces the danger of splitting, and increases the hold of the screw.

The table below shows recommended drill sizes. In very hard woods, or in end grain, it is advisable to make the thread hole slightly larger than the size indicated.

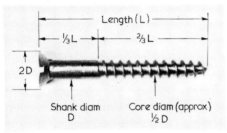

Steel screws are cheapest and strongest. Some woods (eg oak) contain acids; rusting can be avoided by using zinc-plated steel screws.

Lubricate screws with a smear of petroleum jelly or wax.

Screw Gauge No:	0	1	2	3	4	5	6	7	8	9	10	11	12	14	16	18
Clearance Hole Size:	$\frac{1}{16}$	$\frac{5}{64}$	$\frac{3}{32}$	$\frac{7}{64}$	$\frac{1}{8}$	$\frac{9}{64}$	$\frac{5}{32}$	$\frac{11}{64}$	$\frac{3}{16}$	$\frac{13}{64}$	$\frac{7}{32}$	$\frac{15}{64}$	$\frac{1}{4}$	$\frac{17}{64}$	$\frac{9}{32}$	$\frac{5}{16}$
Thread Hole Size:	$\frac{3}{64}$	$\frac{3}{64}$	$\frac{1}{16}$	$\frac{1}{16}$	$\frac{5}{64}$	$\frac{5}{64}$	$\frac{5}{64}$	$\frac{3}{32}$	$\frac{3}{32}$	$\frac{7}{64}$	$\frac{7}{64}$	$\frac{1}{8}$	$\frac{1}{8}$	$\frac{5}{32}$	$\frac{3}{16}$	$\frac{3}{16}$

SOME CONTEMPORARY
BRITISH WOOD SCULPTURE

*(Above) 'Hollow Form with White (Elegy III)' by
Barbara Hepworth (yew), 4ft 5in. Tate Gallery, London*

*(Below) 'Black Cat' by Ferelyth Wills (ebony), 1ft 2in.
By courtesy of I. Henstock; photograph, Charles White*

*(Above) 'Rhythmic Form' by John Skelton (yew), 6ft 7in.
Photograph, John Skelton*

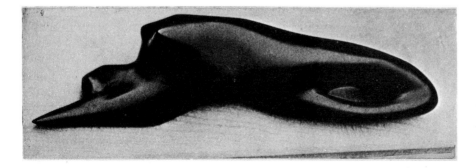

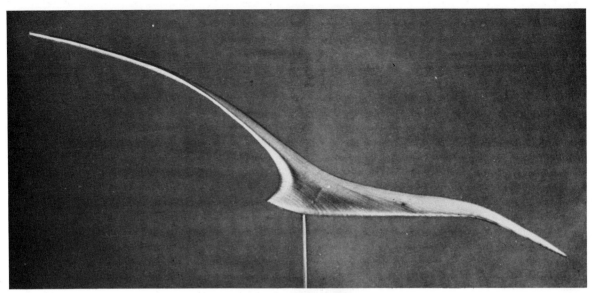

(Above) 'Gull' by John Thorpe (ash), 2ft 9in. By courtesy of M. Beckett

(Below) 'Composition' by Henry Moore (dark African wood), 15in. Photograph by courtesy of Lord Clark

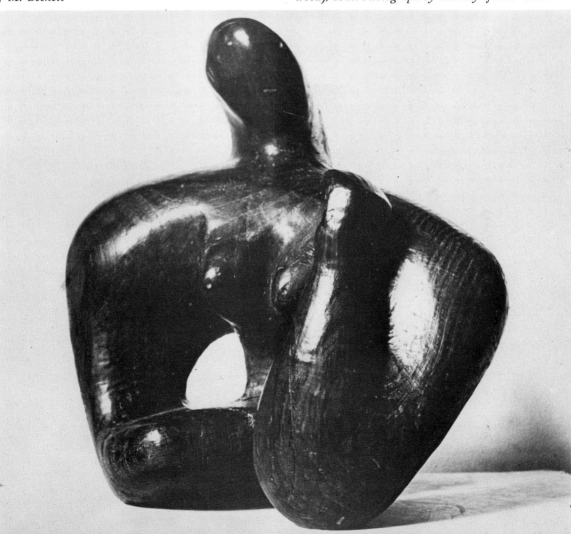

(Above) Statues by John Skeaping from Lincoln Cathedral, on loan from King's College, Cambridge. They represent 'Saint Hugh', 'Christ in Glory' and 'The Virgin Mary'. The figures are 7ft high. By courtesy of the Dean of Lincoln and of King's College, Cambridge.

(Left) 'Torso of Adam' by John Skelton (walnut), 4ft 7in. Photograph, John Skelton

(Below) 'Fiesta' by John Skelton (olive wood), 2ft. Photograph, John Skelton

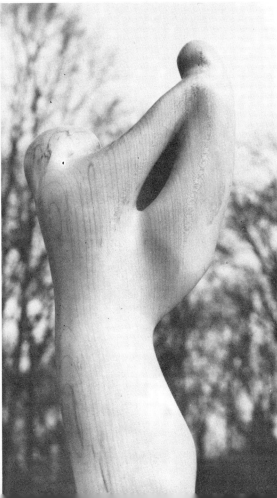

(Above left) 'Head' by Dora Clarke (elm driftwood from the top of an old groyne), 7in. By courtesy of Mrs H. T. Clarke; photograph, A. C. Cooper, London

(Above right) 'Coloured Girl from Massachusetts' by Dora Clarke (rosewood), 12in. Ashmolean Museum, Oxford; photograph, Photo Assignments, London

(Left) 'Mother and Child' by Ferelyth Wills (sycamore), 2ft 9 in. By courtesy of W. I. and R. Massil

(Below) Detail from the statue in Lincoln Cathedral, 'The Virgin Mary' by John Skeaping

(Above) 'Otter' by Ken Wilkinson (Indian laurel with granite base), 8in

(Right) 'Stoat' by George Taylor (ash), 12in

(Below) 'Horse' by John Skeaping. The legs are of pyinkado. The body is of Honduras mahogany and is made in two halves bolted together, hollow. The walls are about 3in thick. It was carved with an adze and is about one and a half times life size. Tate Gallery, London

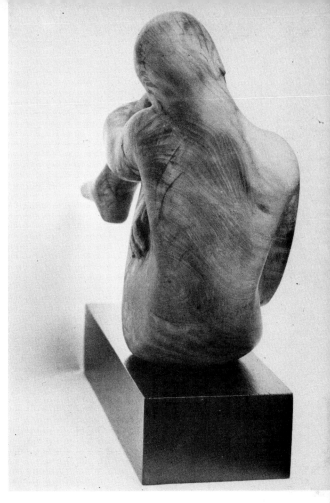

(Above and right) 'Resting Boy' by Dora Clarke (cut from a 3in slice of a 400-year-old yew). By courtesy of Mrs G. Ahern; photograph, Photo Assignments

'Boy, Standing' by Thalia Polak (doussie), 1ft 6in

'Boy, Crouching' by Thalia Polak (yew), 8in

FURTHER READING

It is, of course, impossible to list here all the beautiful art books available. The London Art Bookshop (7 Holland Street, London W8 4NA) specialises in books on art and craft, and will supply a catalogue on request.

The following list will provide a foundation on which to base a wider selection:

SCULPTURE IN GENERAL
BAZIN, G. *The History of World Sculpture* (1970)
HAMMACHER, A. M. *Evolution of Modern Sculpture* (1969)
JAMES, P. (ed). *Henry Moore on Sculpture* (1966)

SCULPTORS
Barbara Hepworth: A Pictorial Autobiography (1970)
Henry Moore: Sculpture and Drawings with an introduction by Herbert Read (1949)

WORKING WITH WOOD
HAYWARD, C. *The Woodworker's Pocket Book* (1968)
HOPPE, H. *Whittling and Woodcarving* (New York, 1969)
MEILACH, D. Z. *Contemporary Art with Wood* (1968)

CRAFTS IN GENERAL
NAYLOR, G. *The Arts and Crafts Movement* (1971)
PORTCHMOUTH, J. *Creative Crafts for Today* (1969)
Crafts magazine, published every two months from 28 Haymarket, London SW1Y 4YZ

LIST OF SUPPLIERS

Most of the tools required can be bought from your local tool shop. Probable exceptions are: (1) woodcarving gouges (don't buy the standard 'beginner's woodcarving set'), sculptor's adze, rifflers and special files for wood; (2) cloth-backed abrasive strip and sheet; (3) leather apron; (4) protective face mask.

(1) Special sculptor's tools can be obtained from:

Alec Tiranti Ltd, 21 Goodge Place,
London W1P 1FD

Alec Tiranti Ltd, Shop and Post Orders,
70 High Street, Theale, Berkshire

who will supply a catalogue on request.

(2) Cloth-backed abrasive strip and sheet. The name and address of your nearest supplier can be obtained from:

3M United Kingdom Ltd, 3M House,
Wigmore Street, London W1A 1ET

(3) Pliable leather aprons are made for the welding trade. For your nearest suppliers try the *Classified Directory* or the telephone directory *Yellow Pages* under 'Industrial Protective Clothing'. They can be obtained, either in person or by post, from:

H. Fisher,
Distributors and Factors (Fareham) Ltd,
85 Manners Road, Southsea, Hants PO4 OBD

(4) Among the many masks obtainable are:

The Martindale Protective Mask
Robinson's Disposable Face Masks.

Both are cheap and effective, and can be bought from most chemists.

OTHER INFORMATION

CRAFT COURSES
Residential weekend, weekly, and vacation courses in all kinds of crafts are available at West Dean College, Chichester, Sussex. Enquiries to The Director.

MUSEUMS AND GALLERIES
A comprehensive list of museums and galleries in Great Britain and Ireland can be obtained from:

ABC Travel Guides Ltd, Oldhill,
London Road, Dunstable LU6 3EB, Beds.

WOOD IDENTIFICATION
If you need help in identifying a particular wood, send your query with a small sample showing the colour and grain figure, stating the approximate measurements of the piece you have, to:

The Building Research Establishment,
Princes Risborough Laboratory,
Princes Risborough, Aylesbury, Bucks